W9-BKL-170

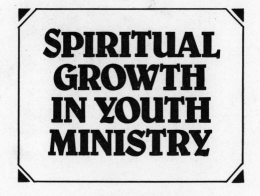

SPIRITUAL GROWTH IN YOUTH MINISTRY

J. DAVID STONE

Group ®
Books

Box 481 • Loveland, CO 80539

Spiritual Growth in Youth Ministry

Designed by Jean Bruns

Library of Congress Cataloging-in-Publication Data

Stone, J. David.
    Spiritual growth in youth ministry.

    Bibliography: p.
    1. Youth—Religious life.   2. Spiritual exercises.   3. Church work with youth.   I. Title.
BV4531.2.S82   1985   259'.23   85-12623
ISBN 0-931529-04-2

Contents

Dedication

To D.L. Dykes Jr., senior pastor emeritus of First United Methodist Church, Shreveport, Louisiana.

You taught me how to apply the Gospel in my life by applying it in yours. You are the inspiration for this book. Thank you, boss.

PART ONE

THE NEED
FOR
SPIRITUAL
GROWTH

A Relational Rationale for Spiritual Growth

What does it mean to be a Christian? That was the question asked a panel of three ministers during a spiritual emphasis week at a small Christian college. I listened intently as the panel attempted to answer the question.

The first minister offered a stuffy response, "Being a Christian means to acquire knowledge of the Christ through God's Word, developing a ritualistic approach of communication with God and acting on that knowledge with courage."

The next minister, in a tone and demeanor that would strike envy among today's television evangelists, said, "To be a Christian is to be washed by the blood of the sacrificial lamb and cleansed forever in the temple of the

Holy Spirit." Then he turned to the last member of the panel and asked, "Isn't that right, Brother Bob?"

Bob was obviously the junior member of the panel of ministers and seemed surprised by the query. Bob blurted out: "I'm not sure I know what either one of you said. When I think of being a Christian, I simply recognize that God loves me and what a tremendous difference that love has made in my life." There was an eruption of thunderous applause and then a standing ovation of approval from the students.

I think this book is like that. It's not a cognitive, theological study of the faith or an attempt to explain who God is or why things work out the way they do. **Spiritual Growth in Youth Ministry** is not designed to be an emotional approach that manipulates the soul of youth. This book simply shares the value of relationships in spiritual growth and how to help those relationships happen. It is also an opportunity to share my own faith journey in youth groups that I have served. **Spiritual Growth in Youth Ministry** is not intended to be a systematic theology. It is not a review of spirituality traditions. This is a practical resource, providing scores of ideas for you to use.

This book is designed to provide structure and models for your personal spiritual growth and your group's spiritual growth. The focus of this resource is practical. It is intended to provide warm and flexible guidance for the development and growth of spirituality for you and your youth group.

I remember my frantic first assignment as a full-time youth director in a church of 1,100 members. I was young, inexperienced, committed to God, enthusiastic and ready to tackle the world. I loved youth! I attended their ballgames, went to their schools, hosted socials, designed fabulous retreats and "hung out" with them. My schedule was always overloaded, my office was never empty, and my family never (well, almost never)

saw me. I was doing youth ministry for God, and it was
working. Youth were everywhere. I was relating! At
least at the time I believed I was relating.

Then one day, a person asked me pointedly and honestly about the focus of my ministry. I felt defensive
and snapped back, "My ministry is Christ-centered, of
course." But just as soon as I had responded, my heart
fell. I began to ask myself the same question. I conned
myself for a while saying, "I may not intentionally try to
center Christ in all my ministry, but I'm 'living' Christ,
showing Christ's love through my actions."

But that answer didn't help. Somehow the question
kept nagging at me until I began to ask myself, "Where
is Christ in what I am doing?" The answer was clear:
While I may have been living Christ, it was almost by
accident—certainly not by intention.

I could not face this new insight. I was devastated. I
had been spending my time running a youth group
"country club," as my critics would say. Although the
statistics were good and the youth were enjoying the
ministry—something was missing. I knew what it was. I
just could not admit that I had been wrong.

The turning point for me came when a good friend
personalized the focus of my ministry by asking, "How
is your walk with the Lord, David?" I felt confronted.
But this time I did not feel defensive. I felt guilty. I had
"found myself" much like the Prodigal Son acknowledged his real self (Luke 15:11-32). My friend's question
cut through all of my pride and ego as I honestly
answered, "I don't know."

I chart that day as the beginning of my spiritual
growth ministry with youth. My youth group continued
to have retreats and parties, and I continued to attend
school functions, but there was a big difference—Christ
really was the center of the youth ministry, because I
had made him the center of my life.

This book may be the most important book I have

written. **Spiritual Growth in Youth Ministry** addresses
head-on the most important need for both teenagers and
youth workers—to grow closer to God the Creator, God
the Savior, and God the Spirit. Building relationships
with young people is the book's primary resource for
catalyzing spiritual growth in youth ministry.

Spiritual Growth in Youth Ministry is personal. Everything in it reflects my years as a growing Christian,
youth worker and family man.

Spiritual Growth in Youth Ministry is practical. All of
the structured models are more than concepts. They
are proven exercises, programs, and projects that have
worked and will work if you are willing to let go and invest yourself. This book is peppered with many ideas
for you to use or adapt. And I've offered guidelines for
adapting them.

Read through the entire book. Highlight those ideas
and concepts that strike you as good starting points. Do
not treat this book as a complete answer for the spirituality needs of you and your youth group. Instead, let it
become a stimulus for fresh, new growth for you in
youth ministry.

—*J. David Stone*

2

The Spiritual Needs of Young People

The young indicate that they want to go deep into the great places of God through prayer, Bible study and personal discipline. Recreation, activities and entertainment are way down on the urgency scale for this generation of God-seekers. Relevance is no longer the code word in the religious quest of youth. Get used to a new word: spirituality.[1]

WHERE ARE YOUNG PEOPLE SPIRITUALLY?

The following quiz reveals substantial research to

[1]George Gallup Jr. and David Poling, **The Search for America's Faith** (Nashville: Abingdon, 1980), p.34.

confirm the quote above from George Gallup Jr. and
David Poling. Take the quiz. You may be surprised by
some of the answers.

A Youth Culture Quiz

TRUE/FALSE

_____ 1. New studies indicate that 95 percent of youth between the ages of 13 to 18 believe in God.

_____ 2. Nine out of 10 youth pray; four out of 10
frequently.

_____ 3. There is movement toward traditional values; for
example, respect for authority and family ties.

_____ 4. A whopping 20 percent of youth today can name
the Ten Commandments; 50 percent can name
five or more.

_____ 5. Of those youth who regularly attend church, two
out of 10 do not know why Easter is celebrated.

_____ 6. Religion does impact the home (helps in family relationships) by a minimum of 45 percent.

_____ 7. Nearly half of youth in the Gallup survey have
said they would respond to requests for their help
in Sunday school, Christian education, youth activities as well as a variety of tasks in social work,
church music, sports programs and fellowship
events.

_____ 8. As many as half of our teenage boys say they
favor a plan of national service to their country
and community in either military or non-military
duty.

_____ 9. At least 20 percent of all people treated for de-
pression are under 18 years old.

_____10. The portion of children in the United States who
live with only one parent has doubled since 1960.

MULTIPLE CHOICE

_____11. The negative attitude of youth toward the organized church is a result of:
   a. failure of the church to genuinely serve the people.
   b. the shallow and superficial stance of many church members.
   c. inability of congregations to appeal to youth on a solid spiritual basis.
   d. absence of excitement or warmth within the church's fellowship.
   e. negative feeling about the clergy in charge.
   f. all of the above.

_____12. The reason(s) people are unchurched is (are) they:
   a. lose their faith.
   b. quit praying.
   c. don't study the Bible anymore.
   d. decide that their children should not have religious instruction from the church.
   e. none of the above.
   f. all of the above.

_____13. If you do not know the answer to a spirituality question, you should tell your youth:
   a. to look it up, it will mean more to them.
   b. that you do not know, but will find out.
   c. stall them until you can get an answer.
   d. refer them to the pastor.

_____14. The *best* way to build community with youth is:
   a. encourage regular Sunday school/CCD attendance.
   b. take retreats.
   c. visit them in their homes.
   d. take trips (choir tours, etc.).

_____ 15. The main thing that youth are looking for in the church is:
a. a Christian recreation program.
b. inclusive activities.
c. spiritual nourishment.
d. dynamite programs on youth problems.
e. a channel for peace and justice endeavors.

_____16. When recruiting volunteers to help in youth ministry:
a. call parents first.
b. put an announcement in the church newsletter.
c. call prospects on the telephone after checking qualifications.
d. ask Sunday school classes to furnish one per quarter.
e. all of the above.
f. none of the above.

_____17. What percentage of teenagers think that drinking is bad for their health and yet still drink?
a. 12
b. 32
c. 42
d. 62

_____18. The leading cause of death among young people 16 to 24 is:
a. drug overdose.
b. drunken driving.
c. suicide.
d. disease (cancer, etc.).

_____19. When beginning a spiritual growth program, the first step must be:
a. form a spiritual growth committee.
b. meet with the pastor.
c. have a personal spiritual growth program.
d. ask some experts to come in and help you get started.
e. have a spiritual growth retreat.

_____20. The most significant role model for most youth is
   a. parent.
   b. youth director.
   c. pastor.
   d. coach or teacher.

See page 216 for the quiz answers.

TWO DECADES AGO

It was the mid-1960s. I was just a couple of years out
of graduate school serving as a youth minister in a
mainline Protestant church in the deep South. Our
youth group was active and growing: Youth met youth,
received "warm fuzzies," carried out some service
projects, and sat together in worship where they wrote
notes and irritated those around them. We always
opened the youth group program with prayer, bowed
our heads in church when the pastor prayed and gave
to the youth mission fund.

At a regular church service during that time, one of
our counselors talked about a "lay witness mission"
that she and her husband had attended. I had heard of
lay witness missions, but did not know quite what to
think. She explained that a group of lay people would
visit a church for a weekend and share their faith in
brief programmed talks. They stayed in church members' homes, hosted prayer and share meetings, and
conducted worship on Sunday. At these services, not
only the visiting laity gave testimonies, but many of the
church members shared the personal ways in which
they had been touched that weekend.

"These people took time from their regular jobs—
they were just ordinary people like us," she said.

That was the first time I had ever really known that

the laity could communicate the Gospel without going to seminary. I must admit that I was more than intrigued; I thought it was a great idea.

The fallout came, however, when I began to see people (myself included) taking sides. Some of the laity in our church who were "converted" began to act as though only they had "the truth." I became defensive. So did my senior pastor. Before we knew it, speaking in tongues, all-night prayer vigils, Bible study and prayer groups became the rage. Our church began to split into those "who had it" (you could tell by the look in their eyes and the tears) and those who did not. I found myself aligned with those who did not have it. In fact, if a person showed any emotion, I simply concluded that individual was *one of those*.

As a reaction to this new trouble, the sermons in our church changed, as did the youth program. We dropped such words as Jesus, Lord and Holy Spirit from our vocabulary. We feared that if we used those words, we might be thought of as *one of those*.

At first I thought that this problem was unique to our congregation. It was not long before I realized that our church was no different from most other congregations. I found that churches across America were going through the same experience. The unfortunate result of this was that spirituality—or what might be called the practice of spirituality—was dropped from many mainline churches and replaced with preaching, programs, projects and parties that left out such words as Jesus, Lord and Holy Spirit. These replacement activities included discourses and programs on Christian behavior and "how to be nice."

In many mainline church youth groups, more emphasis was placed on singing in the choir so that the youth could go on choir tours, or working at the car wash and bake sale so that the youth could go on the trip to Disney World or Six Flags. Increasingly, people avoided spiritual talk so as not to be mislabeled as *one of those.*

Also during the mid-1960s, youth gatherings sponsored by the church became the vogue. Emphasis from the hierarchy was on appearances: No long hair for boys; no short skirts for girls. Youth were not active and youth groups who "had it" were criticizing other youth groups for being "country clubs." The nature of that turbulent decade also led to young people openly challenging the church's preoccupation with itself.

The 1970s saw little emphasis on spiritual growth in youth groups. "Me-ism" was rampant. Youth were taught an unbalanced emphasis on self-love. The "I'm okay, you're okay" mantra was confused with "Love your neighbor as you love yourself."

THE WILDERNESS YEARS

I call the period up to the early 1980s "the wilderness years" in youth ministry. With the apparent split in the mainline church and youth programs reduced to splintered Christianity, it was a sort of "cafeteria Christ"—people picked and chose whatever they wanted. There seemed to be a tremendous lack of leadership. There was no direction. When someone was inspired, his or her words seemed hollow and without substance. Throughout this period, however, there grew a hunger for deeper spirituality.

The move to the social-reform Gospel seemed apparent for so many. After all, did not Christ call us to feed the hungry? Many people watched or participated in programs of concern for the social ills. Workcamps in poverty areas at home and abroad became the rage. As one of the those "doing the Lord's work," I felt as if the Lord was not the prime motivation. Perhaps those of us involved were not *allowing* God to motivate us.

Youth programs gradually moved out of the "wilderness" into a more meaningful direction. In my youth group, I noticed that when we would "ring-up" to pray by putting our arms around each other in a circle, there was a sense of belonging and acceptance that I had not felt before. Acceptance did not come simply by "ringing up." Quite by accident, we were meeting a genuine need to touch and belong that had not been previously addressed. The "ring-up" at the beginning and conclusion of every youth event developed into a ritual. In fact, the "ring-up" became the first identifiable ritual in our group.

Ritual became important in our youth ministry. Although it was accidentally discovered, I realized the importance of providing meaningful and consistent activities. Our youth group was addressing a previously unidentifiable and universal need—the need to belong. Many other rituals followed in our group, and I will outline them later in this book.

Merton Strommen published the results of an ambitious study of more than 7,000 youth in his book **Five Cries of Youth**. In the book, Strommen points out than an overwhelming 75 percent of church youth long to be part of a caring, accepting group.

> *Three out of four want to be a part of a caring, accepting group. Two out of three want a group that, in addition to offering acceptance, also confronts one another with an honest, frank sharing of personal feelings.*[2]

The then popular "human potential movement" was making great strides in helping people identify themselves and learn how to relate through such philosophies as transactional analysis, values clarification or Gestalt. At the same time, however, the human potential movement was taking a lot of flak from some Christian groups as being too "humanistic." Of course, the

---

[2]Merton P. Strommen, **Five Cries of Youth** (New York: Harper & Row, 1974), p. 27.

movement was humanistic, but that's not necessarily bad. Some truths about interpersonal relationships did emerge and are worth keeping.

Probably because of the turbulent 1960s, the research educators overworked their systems to crank out a barrage of statistical data that Strommen corroborated through his own testing in **Five Cries of Youth.** Eighty percent of church youth surveyed had a poor self-image, low self-regard and diminished feeling of self-worth.[3]

I combined some of the principles of the human potential movement with the statistical needs and perceived needs of youth, and moved toward actualizing and personalizing the Gospel in the lives of individuals. I call this concept "lifestyle Christianity." The theme has become: It's the life we live, not the creed we profess, that makes a difference.

The underlying power for lifestyle Christianity is, of course, the Holy Spirit. When lifestyle Christianity came into being in our youth group, I could feel a more complete, realistic and rich involvement of our youth in the life of our church. It was total ministry. It was wholistic. It touched youth were they hurt—anywhere they hurt. It was holistic. God's power was welcomed and became a part of each person's lifestyle. What a deep, abiding and authentic discovery.

For the past several years, I have felt the restlessness of youth in their quest for a viable faith. I have watched them struggle, reach out and stumble on a journey in faith. I have sensed their honest quest and sincere application of Christian principles.

I am finding that the church is beginning to be less threatened by the use of the words Jesus, Lord and Holy Spirit. In fact, it seems that the church is embracing these terms more now, and with more meaning. This

---

[3]Strommen, **Five Cries of Youth,** pp. 26-28.

is a positive time for the authentic church with its
youth. Youth are ready to receive the truth.

SPIRITUALITY—A WORKING DESCRIPTION

The word spirituality conjures up many images. Spirituality has several definitions which range from a
"show me" attitude of the fundamentalist to the "so
what" attitude of the liberal. Spirituality can mean
anything sacred or religious.

For the purposes of this book, I will use a deeper,
more personal definition of spirituality. Spirituality is
not just being aware of specific aspects of or feeling a
closeness with God. It is an articulate closeness to God
demonstrated in the life that you live. You accept God's
gift of life and respond to God in the way that you live
with others. A theological description of this concept is:
"incarnational faith." A less formal way to say it: God
is living in me! "I have been crucified with Christ; . . . I
live by faith in the Son of God . . ." (Galatians 2:20)

Youth want to know how to build a spiritual life.
They want their lives to count. They need to belong and
fit in. If we, as church leaders, can offer them a responsible possibility for spiritual life, they *will* respond
enthusiastically to Christ.

THE BOTTOM LINE . . .

Youth have a need to belong and to be accepted.
They are leaning toward spiritual fulfillment. They
want models. Those of us who work with youth need to
offer a setting that meets their personal, social and
spiritual needs. We must provide role models that are
authentic in both practice and spirit. The youth ministry will astonish even the most cynical as it grows and
becomes the symbol of the power of Jesus Christ. That
contagious fever will affect the youth group's church in
the same ways. "A little child shall lead them" (Isaiah
11:6).

PART TWO

SPIRITUAL GROWTH FOR YOUTH WORKERS

Spiritual Disciplines for Youth Workers

I confess that I have led many "spiritual" Bible studies, prayer groups and youth ministry activities without having been "spiritual" myself. I was doing my job—or at least fulfilling my job description. I often felt selfish and guilty. Perhaps I was, but the results with kids were basically good. What we did was real. I was searching along with my youth group members.

I may have been a good youth leader—but I was a poor student. I lacked the necessary association with my adult peers. Such fellowship and study are absolutely crucial for youth workers. I remember my frustration with youth group kids because some did not seem to think that what we were doing was important. Although I was meeting regularly with the youth group,

I was not demonstrating the importance of study, prayer and sharing in my own life. They perceived I was saying "don't do as I do" but "do as I tell you."

When spiritual disciplines became an integral part of my life, I noticed that the youth were more interested in what I had to say and it seemed that what I said had more credibility. Having my own personal spiritual needs met not only gave me a sense of confidence, but it helped the youth group members realize that Bible study and prayer were not games to play, but honest and sincere searches for God and his wisdom.

A spirituality program for your group depends on your own spirituality. If you do not have a personal spiritual growth program, how can you expect the youth in your ministry to grow spiritually? If you are not participating in an adult prayer or Bible study group, then you cannot expect a youth prayer or Bible study group to flourish. The bottom line: The genesis of anything that really works is at the top. Spiritual growth in youth ministry begins with you.

In this chapter, I will list a number of personal spiritual growth disciplines for youth workers. I recommend that you choose at least one idea to follow for a minimum of 30 days or a maximum of one year. By practicing the discipline at least 30 days, you can produce a routine that will allow for freedom of movement and insight. Eventually, following the discipline will become second nature.

Growing spiritually is similar to what I experiencd when I learned to fly. I remember my confusion as I sat in the cockpit with my instructor. As I looked at the various dials, radios and other instruments, I was overwhelmed with my lack of experience. My instructor told me to place my feet on the rudder pedals, keep my hand on the throttle and tell ground control I was taxiing for takeoff; I briefly felt as if it were more than I could handle. I was excited about learning to fly, but there were so many new dimensions to absorb.

Day after day as I worked diligently to learn, I became more proficient; I worried less about my feet on the rudder pedals. Eventually, my feet "knew" what to do without my having to tell them. I began to understand the pilot lingo that crackled out of the tiny radio speaker. It became natural for me to glance at the oil pressure and temperature gauges. Almost before I knew it, I was ready to solo.

Just as with learning to fly, spiritual disciplines seem awkward at first. A spiritual discipline can interrupt established routines, challenge securities and break into entrenched private habits. I am not suggesting that you need to be afraid to change your routine. I am suggesting that there can be frustration and fear when a dramatic change is initiated. It takes time to re-establish a routine, or more accurately, to develop a ritual. However, once the new ritual is properly established, it becomes entrenched in a lifestyle that has power and produces spiritual growth not only in one's self, but also in others.

Many times, as a result of a "mountaintop experience" or out of a desperation period, well-meaning people decide that they need to pray more or study the Bible more often. They jump into a Bible study or prayer group, or decide to rise at 5 a.m. to have a quiet time with God. That is admirable! After a period of time, however, the excitement and fascination of the new-found discipline wear off and leave a feeling of guilt when attempts are made to change gears or stop the discipline altogether. These people burn out by trying to change too much too soon.

To avoid this potential problem, I recommend that you set parameters. Before you begin any personal discipline, determine when it will end or what you will move to next. Parameters will give you an opportunity to become familiar with the model, but not defeat you or make you feel guilty when you stop. You will have a feeling of accomplishment and a sense of spiritual growth at the conclusion. If your discipline has produced desired results and has become a ritual, renegotiate with yourself for more time. Build your spiritual growth activity in blocks of time, not marriages of forevers.

THE LISTENING POST

When Dr. E. Stanley Jones came to my town, I was given the responsibility of being his host, taxi driver and valet. I was a little incensed that I (with a master's degree in Christian education and a responsible job as director of youth ministry in a prestigious downtown church) should be asked to do such menial tasks as drive Dr. Jones to his meetings. I was not aware that Dr. Jones was the author of more than 30 books, a renowned speaker and minister, had the humbleness of a saint and the demeanor of Jesus. Little did I know that he would profoundly impact my life. He practiced what he preached. He *was* what I saw. My contact with him was a turning point in my ministry.

That first morning, Dr. Jones was to speak at a prayer breakfast and I was to deliver him. I was not too happy. I had to get up at 5:30 a.m., hurriedly dress, and drive for 20 minutes to the hotel where he was staying. I was further exasperated when at 6:20 my knock on his door brought no response. I persisted, checked the coffee shop and returned to his room at 6:30 to knock again. Much to my surprise, the door swung open and Dr. Jones warmly greeted me; he was ready to go. I recounted to him that I had knocked earlier but received no response. He explained that he probably did not hear the knock because he was at his "listening post." I just shrugged and said, "Oh." I had not wanted to admit that I did not know what a "listening post" was because Dr. Jones had said it so matter-of-factly.

About midday, my curiosity got the better of me. As we were riding to the next commitment, I asked about the "listening post." Dr. Jones turned to me and said: "I wish you had asked me earlier, and I would have shown you. When you take me in tonight, I will show you." I thanked him; my curiosity was even more rampant. I wondered, "What in the world is a 'listening post'?"

By 11 p.m. not only had I realized that I was in the presence of a most saintly man, I was intrigued, enlightened, inspired and tired. I also was excited because I finally was going to learn about the "listening post."

Dr. Jones opened the door to his room, pointed to a corner and said, "There it is." All I could see was an old pillow. Dr. Jones explained that the pillow was special and had come from India. Each morning from 6 to 6:30, he would kneel on the pillow with his back erect, eyes closed and palms turned upward. Then he would listen, listen, listen.

Dr. Jones asked, "Have you ever thought that most of the time when we try to get in touch with God, we do all the talking?" He explained, "I just sit at my listening post for 30 minutes each day and listen for God to direct me."

It sounded so simple. I could hardly wait to get home and try it. I had such a longing to *really* make contact with God. I crawled into the bed that night full of anticipation of my 30 minutes alone with God the next morning at my "listening post."

My excitement woke me 30 seconds before my alarm sounded. I thought perhaps God woke me before the alarm sounded. I quickly turned it off, slipped into my robe and slippers, and quietly made my way into the den. I used one of the corduroy pillows for my "special" pillow. I placed it on the floor next to a window, knelt with my body erect, closed my eyes, turned my palms upward and began my 30 minutes of listening to God. As the minutes went by, I kept waiting for God to say something. I heard nothing. At least nothing from God. I did hear the house creak, a train rumble by in the distance, one of my daughters cough and other usual morning sounds. I was discouraged. During the entire 30 minutes, I was in sheer agony: my bare knees were being cut by those little razor edges of the corduroy, my back hurt, my arms felt as if they were about to drop off. I only sensed that God was present for perhaps 10 seconds. It did not seem worth it.

When I picked up Dr. Jones later that morning, he seemed more excited than ever when he asked, "How'd it go?"

I reluctantly replied: "Not so good. I think that I only heard God for about 10 seconds in the whole 30 minutes."

Dr. Jones exclaimed: "That's great! The first time I ever tried it, all I could hear were trains, the house creaking and other outside noises."

And I shouted, "Me too!"

"It was several days before I was able to focus on God. It took me years to be able to concentrate enough to hear God for the full 30 minutes," said Dr. Jones.

Then I began to wonder if I had heard God at all. I heard all those other sounds and thought that I just wasn't in tune.

Dr. Jones continued to explain: "Have you ever thought from where those sounds come? The engineer on that train is of God, the train was taking goods to God's people. The limb scratching across the top of the house is of God. All sounds are from God. When we recognize those sounds are from God, then we can begin to focus on him."

With his encouragement, I decided to set aside 30 minutes a day for 90 days to experiment with my newly found "listening post." I never reached the point at which I could hear God for the whole time, but the 30 minutes became special to me. I felt God's presence during the majority of the time. The "listening post" really works, but you must strive to make it happen.

Any time is a good time to begin this discipline; there will never be a "perfect" time. If you want to experience the "listening post," here is a plan:

1. Set aside several minutes a day. First, choose a special place where you will have a minimum of interruptions. It may be the living room, den or bedroom. Consider this your special place where you eventually will develop a structured communication with God.

In this place, you will need a pillow on which to kneel. Plan for a time when you will have the most solitude. Establish a routine, for example: When the alarm goes off, roll out of bed immediately, put on your house clothes, make the coffee, put the cat out, go to your special place, kneel on your pillow and listen.

2. Listen. At first you will hear every possible sound. Part of the reason is that many people never stop long enough to "listen to life" or to "smell the roses." Listening involves focusing. It is difficult to focus on one sound when there are so many different noises. One way to sort through the many noises is to choose one sound and concentrate on how it is made. Think about how God is involved in that sound. Put yourself into that sound and mentally repeat: "Here am I, Lord. Speak to me."

If your mind starts to wander, bring it back by concentrating on that sound again. Do not be discouraged if you do not feel the presence of God immediately.

3. Be faithful to your discipline. Stick with it. In the beginning, establish that you are going to participate in the spiritual discipline for a particular period of time, then do not miss. Consider it your appointment with God. You would not think of breaking an appointment with someone else, so certainly do not break your appointment with God.

Over the years, I have gone to my "listening post" as

a personal discipline and found the benefits to be exceptional. Even if you discontinue your "listening post," you can easily return with just a little practice.

PRAYER

We pray because we need to pray just as we need to sleep and eat. We should not pray because we feel guilty or obligated. We should not pray because we are expected to as a part of our jobs. Prayer must be a part of our lives. We must live life, not let life live us. Prayer must be an attitude such as Paul talked about, "Rejoice always, pray constantly, give thanks in all circumstances; for this is the will of God in Christ Jesus for you" (1 Thessalonians 5:16-18).

The backbone of any prayer life is to have a ritual of praying at a specific time and place each day. I emphasize "each day" because we need prayer daily just as we should bathe daily. Sometimes we do not feel unclean, but we are. We need the refreshing bath of God's love and guidance each day. Mechanical aspects of prayer such as a set time and place ensure that prayer will be a regular part of our schedules. Call this set, regular prayer time "my time." "My time" means that at 6 a.m. I will arise, go to *my place* and have *my time* with God.

Another mechanical aspect of prayer is posture. Some people say that a person cannot adequately pray unless a kneeling position is assumed and the eyes are closed. When you are deciding how to pray, let these questions be your guide:

● Is the way I am positioned showing humbleness toward God?

● Am I alone with God? Does this place allow me to be private and personal with God with no other interference?

If you can answer "Yes" to these questions, then your posture, time and place are right for you.

Generally, there are two types of prayer: SOS and disciplined.

SOS prayers are offered in a crisis when the proper groundwork has not been prepared through a regular discipline. An SOS prayer is similar to a last-minute desperation pass in a football game. People just throw the prayer "up there" and hope that God catches it. This illustration is not to suggest that God will not "catch" this type of prayer. God hears *all* prayers. This analogy does suggest that our spiritual life is lacking if it only consists of last-minute desperation prayers. Our lives must contain a regular prayer discipline so that when emergencies do arise, we can meet the challenge.

The following story illustrates this point. For several years, Gandy, a goose, flew south for the winter and returned to Canada for the summer. One year, as Gandy's flock was flying low because of the fog, a hunter shot and wounded Gandy. Gandy escaped capture, but could not keep up with the flock because his wing was broken. Gandy was fortunate because he landed near a farm where there were lots of chickens and a friendly farmer.

While Gandy's wing mended, he ate with the chickens and slept at night in the chicken house.

The winter passed. One day Gandy's flock flew over the farm as they returned home. The lead goose called down to Gandy, "Come on, Gandy, we're going home." Gandy looked up, waved goodbye to the chickens and began to flap his wings for takeoff. He was a little too fat for the weak wing to lift him. So Gandy stayed another year.

The next year when the geese flew over, the lead goose called down, "Gandy, come on, we're going home!" Gandy did not even look up.

Gandy's story can happen to us. When we are out of the habit of praying and are enthralled with our own thing, we do not even hear God calling to us; but he is.

Disciplined prayer is a regular, consistent, daily habit. It is living our lives as a prayer. When the emergencies in life come, we know how to make contact and are confident of the results.

There are two basic types of disciplined prayer: verbal and non-verbal. The spoken prayer or verbal prayer is more common. Meditation or non-verbal prayer is the other.

Meditation or non-verbal prayer is an important ingredient in our prayer life. I do not let it take the place of the spoken prayer but let it serve as a transition between the regular prayer times. For example, after having listened to God in my early-morning prayer time, I let those moments become part of my day by recalling them as I meet my daily agenda.

The people driving along side of me in the morning traffic or the grouch on the airplane across the aisle from me become targets of my non-verbal prayers. I simply focus on them as God's children in a meditative, non-verbal way. I used to be amazed how that seemed to change them. Finally I realized that *I* was the one being changed. What a difference it is to be in control of my attitude toward others. I also believe God does indeed change people. And God can do it without me needing to speak even one word.

As we continue to focus on the individual, we will limit this discussion to personal spoken prayers. When you pray, do so with some structure and organization. For example, create a prayer list everyday and pray for each item on the list.

Another example of structure is to use the acronym ACTS. ACTS is a reminder that prayer is actual:

A stands for adoration,

C for confession,

T for thanksgiving, and

S for supplication or petition.

Adoration is praising God. Each morning during my

prayer time, I try to think of all that God is to me: powerful, all-knowing, loving. In my prayer, I affirm these attributes as they pertain to my life situations.

Confession is telling God about my shortcomings. Although God already knows my sins, my admission takes the shortcomings out of the closet and makes me personally vulnerable to God. By sincerely articulating my sins, they become real; then God hears, answers and cleanses me. It is wonderful to have someone who listens and forgives.

Roland Bainton tells a story about Martin Luther that illustrates the need to confess sins.[1] As a Catholic, Martin Luther would go to confession and spend hours confessing all the sins that he had committed. He even mentioned "omissions" most of us would consider inconsequential such as stepping on a live plant. Martin wanted so much to be God's person and tried diligently to accomplish that. When he was through confessing his sins, he would bid the priest goodbye and depart for home. However, on his way home, he often would think of another sin that he forgot to confess and hurry back to the confessional to complete that discipline. I can imagine one priest saying to another: "Oh no, here comes Martin again. You take him this time!"

As extreme as this story seems, a calming and "okay-ness" come with our confession to God.

Thanksgiving is joyful. Saying thank you to God for all things is a seemingly meager way of appreciating the Lord. Yet, God accepts that; and I have a sense of doing something for God for a change. To thank God for my state of being and answered prayer is to more firmly establish God as the source of all power and as giver of all gifts. Thanksgiving builds confidence in my own enunciation of God.

Supplication or petition is necessary as a final part

---

[1]Roland Bainton, **Here I Stand: A Life of Martin Luther** (Nashville: Abingdon, 1978).

of any prayer. After I have acknowledged God as creator, sustainer of life, all powerful and knowing; confessed my sins and shortcomings to him; thanked God for the ways my life has been touched and healed; then I am ready psychologically, emotionally and cognitively to ask for God's help. I have the confidence and the assurance that my prayer not only will be heard, but answered. I offer simple petitions such as: "Lord, help me face my appointment with the banker. Show me what is best for me. Give me the words to say."

The following is an example of one of my prayers using the acronym ACTS:

A "Gracious God, I come into your presence with such timidity, knowing of your power and how separated we are right now. And yet, I do feel your presence in my life and the wonder of your understanding of me. You haven't abandoned me.

C "I love this life you have given me, but I feel so inferior and afraid at times to really launch out. I know what I should be doing, yet can't get hold of it. I am not taking care of my body the way I should. My study and prayer times are not what they should be, and I long to be lifted up. I know you are the only one who can do that. I know that it must begin with me! I need to spend some personal time with each of my daughters. I rationalize that they are too busy or I am. I have not followed up with so many people with whom I need to say thank you.

T "Lord, I want to begin with you. Thank you for your patience with me—for allowing me to stray from your presence and never leaving me. Thank you, God, for this time of year in which I can get refreshed. Your constant love is never ending. I can feel that. Thank you for being available, for caring for me and picking me up when I fall. I am so glad you love me.

S "Gracious Lord, I need your help in the completion of this book. Please give me the right words to say to communicate the heartfelt need that I know youth workers have. Help me, God, to recall experiences and systems that have worked in building spirituality in youth groups. Please help me articulate the truth. Then, God, help me make time for my daughters that I might be the example that you want me to be.

"Finally, Lord, forgive me for being so presumptuous. I want your will for my lfie. I don't want to ever lose you. Show me like never before what I need to do to come closer to you. For it is in the awe, wonder and amazement that I pray to you through Jesus Christ, my example. Amen."

Although disciplined prayer is basic to ensure that the spiritual communion becomes ingrained in your lifestyle, other prayer times are unlimited. The more you are aware of God's presence, the more opportunity you have to communicate. The more you communicate, the more apt you are to do the will of God. The more you do the will of God, the happier you will be! So pray without ceasing! Let God influence you at every turn. Before you go into the office for a confrontation with the boss, say quietly to yourself, "Help me, Lord." Before talking or counseling with a teenager about a problem, ask God for guidance. Before making a decision concerning a job or relationship, call on God to assist you. While jogging or riding in a car, thank God for those around you. Ask God to be present with them. Notice God's handiwork and say thank you. Have an attitude of gratitude. Prayer changes things; it is our lifeline to God.

A caution about trying to build a prayer life: Don't let it overwhelm you. You will quickly become discouraged if you do not realize that the inner self and prayer life must be cultivated. That means the seed does not pop up into a full-grown plant the day it is planted.

On a family vacation one summer to cousin Joe's farm in Illinois, Joe explained to the amazement of my daughter Mitzi (then 4 years old) how corn grows. He gave her an ear of corn and told her to plant a kernel when we got home. Of course, we did, even before we unpacked the car. I can remember explaining to Mitzi that once the corn kernel was safely planted, it would have to be watered and fertilized, and then we would have to allow the sun to help it grow.

Early the next morning, I was awakened by Mitzi tugging at my pajamas and crying, "Daddy, Daddy, it didn't work." She had awakened that morning with the anticipation that the kernel would be grown into a beautiful mature cornstalk. It was a difficult task explaining to her that the little piece of corn was putting out roots; and when it was strong enough, it would push a shoot up through the ground. Mitzi wanted to dig it up and see.

The happiest day came a couple of weeks later when I was awakened again by Mitzi who exclaimed, "It did it, Daddy, it did it!"

Prayer life is similar to this illustration. It takes time to cultivate an attitude of understanding and awareness of the presence of God. We must be faithful. Though we cannot see our attitude grow, it is just like the seed spreading its roots.

Just as we must not let prayer overwhelm us, neither should we pray half-hoping prayers. If we are going to pray for rain, then we should bring an umbrella. We know that whatever we ask in prayer will be done, if we have faith. You might feel more comfortable, however, if you don't begin with big prayer requests. Begin simply such as praying to get rid of a headache, saying, "God, help me to focus on something else and let this headache disappear." Then focus on something else and allow God to answer that prayer. Pray for God to give you the words to say when visiting a friend who has just lost a loved one. God will! Gradually move to bigger prayer requests. You will pray for things believing that God really will answer your prayers. And God will!

BIBLE STUDY

And there are also many other things which Jesus did, the which, if they should be written every one, I suppose that even the world itself could not contain the books that should be written. Amen (John 21:25, KJV).

I had finished my recitation with very little prompting, and the Bible Memory Association members applauded. I had successfully quoted the entire book of John, King James Version. My trip to the BMA camp was secure. I won a brand-new Scofield Reference Bible, and my parents were proud.

I was 12 years old and had just completed a year of Bible memory exercises. I had worked hard, two days a week, learning the names of the books of the Bible, memorizing selected passages from the New Testatment and finally committing the entire book of John to memory.

That was more than 35 years ago. I still remember some of those verses, but what stands out the most is that I did not learn what the verses meant or their origins. I could quote John 3:16 or even a more obscure verse such as John 17:1. I just could not interpret a verse or apply it to life.

My time was not totally wasted memorizing verses of scripture—even today I can recall many of those verses. But I have often thought how much better it would have been to participate in an in-depth study of the Bible.

To establish a better understanding of God's Word, memorization must be accompanied with study: Take a few courses in biblical history, learn biblical concepts and philosophies, establish a better understanding of personalities in the Bible and modern-day Christians in crisis. When we see how others have handled life's situations, we can better understand the living Word of God.

In recent years, I have developed a greater appreciation of the Bible and have allowed it to have a more profound influence on my life. I relate better to the Bible when I accept it as a sacred library of ancient books about people and their encounters with God. The people of the Bible bear witness to the works of God in their lives.

Usually a personal Bible study is undertaken because of a desire to know more about God and his encounters with his people. Sometimes, a Bible study is initiated because of a perceived need to be "religious." For whatever reason you begin, be honest with yourself and make a contract for specific times of study. I recommend you set aside a minimum of one hour a week for study: not Bible reading, Bible study.

Robert McAfee Brown's book **The Bible Speaks to You** has helped me establish a few rules for study.[2] The following points are my paraphrases and explanations of some of Brown's rules:

1. **Trust God's Spirit to reveal his truth.** I never like to argue with people about God's Word or use scripture passages to substantiate who is right or wrong. If I come to the Bible with an open and alert mind and am ready to accept what the Holy Spirit offers, then that revelation will be true and mine. It does not matter what others say. No one can have the exact same

---

[2]Robert McAfee Brown, **The Bible Speaks to You** (Philadelphia: Westminster Press, 1978), pp. 31-51.

thoughts and feelings that I have. No one else has "walked in my shoes" and thus would not experience God's Holy Spirit the same way I do.

Robert Grant, in his book **The Bible in the Church**, quotes Martin Luther:

> *No one can understand Virgil in the Bucolics and Georgics, unless for 5 years he has been a shepherd or farmer. No one understands Cicero in the Epistles (so I presume), unless for 20 years he has held some important office in the state. No one should think he has sufficiently tasted the Holy Scriptures, unless for a hundred years he has governed churches with prophets.*[3]

When you read, read for yourself. Be alert, open and ready for God to speak the truth in light of your experiences.

2. Recognize the individuality of each of the biblical writers. If, in fact, you agree the Bible is a collection of books about man's experiences with God and that the writers lived at different times and in different circumstances, then you must view those writings through their eyes.

Understanding Paul's life as he was writing from prison is similar to closing your eyes and feeling the message of a musician as you listen to a song. It's like looking at a painting on the wall and not trying to analyze it, but allowing the painting to reach out to you with its message. The individual writer's stories may vary due to each author's experiences, training and cultural influences. Nonetheless, the stories are true because they are told from the writer's perspective.

3. Do not attempt to modernize scriptural words. We must seek to discover the meanings of ancient biblical

---

[3]Robert Grant, **The Bible in the Church** (New York: Macmillan, 1948), p. 112.

words in light of what they meant at the time they were written. As time goes on, words change and take on new meanings. To aid in the correct interpretation of scripture, go to the church library or a Christian bookstore and get a good commentary. Read the commentary along with your Bible; this will help keep you close to God's Word and lift you to new heights of insight.

4. **The primary meaning of a passage is the simplest and most natural interpretation.** God's Word is not complicated. We make it complicated by thinking in abstract terms using allegories and symbols. Sometimes, we try to second-guess God or make the Word be what we want it to be. We rationalize and make something difficult out of something that is simple. When Jesus taught, he told stories to illustrate his points. In reading that "Jesus wept," why not just assume he cried? Get inside that emotion instead of trying to ascertain its religious and cataclysmic significance.

5. **View each part of the Bible as a part of the "big picture"—the whole.** Almost every book in the Bible reflects God's redemptive activity on behalf of humanity as we study the Old Testament and read some of the cruel events we ascribe to God, we can recognize the truths of those passages as part of the transformation of God's people.

Only experience in personal Bible study can show when and how to apply these five points. The artist with his brush, paint, canvas and model goes to work in his studio. He positions the model, chooses the colors and begins to paint according to his interpretation. There are no two paintings alike, only imitations. Such is Bible study. Given the tools and space with which to work, we set about learn, grow and be inspired. We must be content to allow time for those things to happen. If we persist, God's Word will "be made flesh" in our lives with one another.

When beginning a Bible study, one of the most common questions is, "Where do I begin?" Several years ago a large Protestant church planned an emphasis on personal Bible study. Since there were so many Bible study books on the market and no one seemed to know which one to begin with, the planning committee came up with a unique idea. The church circulated a letter to each member asking the following question: "If you could pick out five scripture passages that mean the most to you and you would want your family to learn, what would they be?"

The response was incredible. All the answers were tabulated and the top 23 entries were published in the church newsletter. This was a good beginning place for Bible study because the members had been involved in the selection and each of the passages was special. Their list may be a possible beginning point for you in your personal Bible study. Each day choose one of the following verses and reflect on how it applies to your life:

Exodus 20:1-17	Luke 15:11-24
Psalm 23	Luke 15:25-32
Psalm 100	Luke 19:1-10
Psalm 139	John 13:34-35
Micah 6:6-8	John 14:1-17
Matthew 5:1-12	Acts 3:1-10
Matthew 5:13-16	Romans 12:1-21
Mark 4:1-9	1 Corinthians 13
Mark 8:27-36	Ephesians 4:1-6
Mark 10:17-22	Philippians 4:10-13
Mark 10:46-52	Colossians 3:12-17
Luke 10:25-37	

Before you begin your Bible study, visit your pastor or a close Christian friend. Ask him or her to suggest a list of favorite passages or to recommend Bible study books.

If you want to grow spiritually, then plan for a discipline of regular Bible study that will help make the scripture meaningful to you.

In **The Christian Agnostic**, Dr. Leslie D. Weatherhead writes that sometimes we study material that does not seem to fit. He suggests that we not throw the material out, but put it into a drawer labeled "Awaiting Further Light."[4]

I like that idea. There have been times when the material I was reading and studying seemed to be inappropriate or irrelevant to my present situation. However, at a later date, the material proved to be helpful and illuminating.

SPIRITUAL FRIEND

Through the years, prayer, Bible study, share group participation and regular worship have been important to me. But never has anything been as powerfully important as having a spiritual friend.

I first heard the term "spiritual director" many years ago when a Catholic friend remarked he was going to his spiritual director. For a long time after that, I thought a spiritual director was reserved for nuns and priests. Then at a Catholic retreat house near Tampa, Florida, I found that anyone can have a spiritual director. Clergy and laity alike attended that retreat house to be directed in their spiritual journey. As I talked to some of the participants, they clarified the role and purpose of a spiritual director. Spiritual directors usually are designated by people who feel they needed spiritual direction. A person's spiritual director helps him or her grow spiritually by occasionally asking, "How's your walk with the Lord?" A spiritual director guides a person by offering suggestions of scripture to read or books to study.

---

[4] Dr. Leslie D. Weatherhead, **The Christian Agnostic** (Nashville: Abingdon, 1979).

I thought: "What a neat idea! Why hadn't I heard about this before?" New possibilities for my youth group were flashing through my head.

"I can divide my youth group into pairs and let them be spiritual friends for each other. (I decided to use the term 'friend' instead of 'director' since a 'spiritual director' is often a trained professional.) I can ask each church board member to adopt at least one youth member and be his or her spiritual friend. I can conduct spiritual friend workshops within the church and train everyone to be there for each other."

The list seemed almost endless. The idea of a spiritual friend was new to me. I didn't realize that Christians have been doing this throughout the centuries.

Most of us get so wrapped up in helping everybody else in their spiritual growth that ours becomes stagnant. The concept of having a spiritual friend became more personal for me and consequently took on exceptional significance one night in Madison, Wisconsin, following a youth ministries workshop. I was relaxing with a fellow team member, Jim Kolar. I had become close friends with Jim and felt a kinship of faith and understanding. Jim began telling me about his spiritual friend. I thought: "If I know of anyone who is spiritual, it's Jim! He seems to have his whole life together. Why would he need a spiritual friend? What does a spiritual friend do?"

Jim told me he had been directed to meditate on certain scripture passages. He explained that his spiritual friend also served as a confidant to him. Jim was being totally open with me. His honesty was refreshing; I thought I was the only person in church work who had problems. I always had believed people in church work were not supposed to have problems. Unexpectedly, I was listening to my friend share his life with me. I hungered for the opportunity to be able to share with someone in that kind of way without feeling inferior or put down.

Before I could ask Jim if he would be my spiritual friend, he asked, "Well, David, how is your walk with the Lord?" I flushed. He had just nailed me. To look inside yourself is one thing, but to articulate it to someone else is quite another! It is difficult and scary.

As I reflect back to that night years ago, I realize that discussion had a great impact on my own ministry. Each of us needs someone. Over the years, Jim has been my spiritual friend. Each time we get together, I know he is going to ask, "How's your walk with the Lord?" It keeps me focused on Jesus and challenges me to greater heights.

Recently, I was conducting a series of spirituality workshops. One of the workshops was in Minneapolis. Jim lived in nearby St. Paul, so I called him. He did not ask the standard question. I remember my relief—I was feeling guilty because of my lack of spiritual growth and was embarrassed to admit it. He invited me to dinner and offered to drive. During the ride to his home, he still did not ask. We ate a wonderful dinner and discussed our ministries and families. I met his children for the first time; we had an enjoyable visit. I just knew that on the way back to the hotel Jim would ask me about my walk with the Lord, but he did not. At 10 p.m., we pulled into the parking lot at the hotel. I began to say goodbye, but Jim said: "Wait. How's your walk with the Lord?" I knew it. By midnight I had told him. What a release! What joy! What freedom!

Although it can be difficult to share such personal insights, we need someone there to listen. Here are some steps to take in finding a spiritual friend for your life:

1. **Make a list of at least five people.** Choose Christian friends who you feel close to and with whom you would be willing to be vulnerable. You might find it helpful to cultivate someone by first risking your own vulnerability. It is not easy to share yourself; however,

if you risk vulnerability, you gain freedom. Make it as safe as you can, but take a risk. Rank the names on your list in order of your closeness to them:

1. _Steve_
2. _Rhonda_
3. _Karen_
4. _Cindy_
5. _Bill_

2. **Make an appointment.** Schedule a time to visit the person you selected as your first choice. Then keep the appointment. When you go to see someone, it accentuates the importance of your need. The person will think, "This must really be important if he is willing to take the time to make an appointment and come to see me about it."

3. **Explain what you need.** Talk about what you want and describe the role of a spiritual friend. Provide him or her with the following description:

As My Spiritual Friend, You Will . . .

A. Make appointments with me to inventory my spiritual life.

B. Counsel and assign me exercises to follow until the next meeting. (Meetings can be as infrequent as four times a year, or as often as once a month.)

C. Ask me questions such as:

● How is your walk with the Lord?

● How is God active with you in your family? work? church?

● What is the next step you need to take to grow in your walk with the Lord?

D. Give suggestions that have helped with your own spiritual growth such as:

● spiritual readings,

● Bible study exercises,

● prayer disciplines,

● journaling.

4. Establish a one-year commitment. Both you and your spiritual director should promise to maintain the program for a year. Explain that if the person accepts, he or she is to follow the previous description and hold you accountable during that year.

It is important to establish this commitment. Trying to be your own spiritual friend is a lot like the frustration you might have experienced trying to teach your own child an activity such as swimming. You might have found it difficult to be objective because of the closeness between you and your child.

Attempting to be your own spiritual friend is a lot like that. You could ask yourself all the questions a spiritual friend would ask, but you probably would find it difficult to be objective with yourself. A trusted friend, however, will keep you honest and help keep you from rationalizing. Besides, you need someone to continually probe and encourage you so that you do not get stagnant in your faith.

WORSHIP

"I really didn't feel like going to church today," I said. "So I didn't go."

"You missed the best Sunday ever," replied my friend. "Today, when the pastor began his sermon, he told about the songs they used to sing in the little church he grew up in. You know he can't carry a tune, but he just started in a devotional tone singing: 'Oh, how I love Jesus. Oh, how I love Jesus . . .'

"Before I knew it, a few people in the congregation joined in with him, then one after another choir member began to sing. The organist found the pitch, and for the first time at the 11 a.m. worship service, everyone was singing, 'Oh, How I Love Jesus.'

"We sang other old songs, too, such as: 'Blessed Assurance' and 'The Old Rugged Cross.' I'm telling you, it was a religious experience!"

Well, there I was. I had been faithfully attending
church for years, and the first time I decided not to go,
I missed a once-in-a-lifetime experience.

Regular worship is important. You never know when
an extra special day is going to occur. It has been said
that the best time to go to church is when you do not
feel like it. I am convinced of this. We must be available
if God is going to break into our lives. We should never
question church attendance—it should be a weekly
ritual.

In addition to regular weekly worship, I suggest you
have a time to explore other worship possibilities. In
every community there are worship opportunities that
are different from regular morning worship: The Bible
Church sponsors a prominent singer to perform in the
community; the Baptist church holds a revival; the Catholic church conducts a guitar mass. Each month, choose
to attend a different worship service. You will be welcome and, even more importantly, you will enlarge your
worship horizons.

There is always a degree of fear related to trying a
new experience or event. There will always be someone
cautioning you against going to "that church" because
of its theology. Do not completely ignore the caution, but
go with an open mind and heart ready to allow God to
speak to you. God is big enough for everyone. He is big
enough to allow you to discover a truth here, there and
everywhere.

JOURNALS

Have you ever run across an old church bulletin on
which you had scribbled a note to someone? Have you
ever found your old diary in a trunk or read through a
letter written to you long ago? Your thoughts may have
been, "How could that have mattered?" or "Look how
far I've come!"

Keeping a journal is like that. It is writing a letter or

diary to yourself. It is also great fun to later look back and see where you have been. Another tremendous benefit to journaling is that it can encourage you and challenge you to move on. Keeping a journal of your own spirituality is a real adventure and promises long-lasting results.

I went through a period of time in my third full-time, church-related job thinking that God and everyone else had abandoned me. Things were not going right. I was in the middle of moving my family to still another home—probably searching for happiness. As I was packing the same old boxes that I had packed so many times before, I came across an old journal. As I read through the pages, I was captivated, especially with the following entry:

> *Tonight was special. Woody told me after my sermon that he wanted to live the rest of his life serving God. He said it was because of what he had seen in me, and he thanked me for letting God control my life. I am stunned. I feel so humble. God seems to be present with me right now. Thank you, God.*

After reading that entry, I was jolted back to reality. I began to reflect on what was different in my ministry. I had been leaving out God.

One of the best personal spiritual disciplines may be that of keeping a journal. If you journal regularly, you will have a good record of the past, and also a chart of growth.

Most of us fail to keep a daily record of feelings, impressions, and struggles because of rationalizations and excuses. We can't find paper and pencil. The telephone seems to ruin our best intentions. We allow family or business concerns to usurp the time we set aside for journaling. We rationalize that we will write it down "next time." The fallacy of "next time" is that it never comes. The root of all these problems is a failure to set a daily time and stick with it. Follow these steps for journaling:

1. **Decide you are going to do it.** Choose a specific time and place. As with all spiritual disciplines, choosing a specific time and place helps create a habit—a ritual. Also set parameters, "I'll begin January 15 and conclude March 15." Make journal entries *everyday* even if it is, "Dear journal, I don't have time today."

2. **Choose a model of journaling.** There are many models from which to choose. Six examples of journaling are at the end of this section. Decide which best suits you.

3. **Get a notebook.** A standard notebook is best because it fits with the size of other books. Clearly label the notebook as a journal. Do not use it for anything else. In that way, it will become more personal and special. Duplicate the journal model you chose in the previous step.

4. **Do not limit your entries.** Always allow at least one full page for each day of the month. Use as much space as needed; however, begin each day on a new page.

5. **Plan how you will make your entries.** For example, decide the order in which you will make your entries. Several ideas on the following pages could get you started.

6. **Get your thoughts together.** Regardless of the style of entry you have decided to make, when you sit down in "your" place to write, pause long enough to get your thoughts together. Once you are comfortable, close your eyes, take a deep breath and let it out slowly. Repeat this three times. As you do this, think back over your day. Open your eyes and immediately write the thoughts that come to mind. Then follow that entry with answers to the questions from the style of journaling you chose.

7. **Chart your growth.** The Inner Introspection journal model which follows includes a scale to help you chart your spiritual growth. Whatever model you select, design a similar scale to chart your spiritual growth.

Model One: Inner Introspection. This journaling model is a general style of deep introspection that probes the specifics of living out a relationship with God. If followed daily and charted accurately, the personal spiritual growth pattern will always reflect an improving relationship to God. The rationale is that the more we get to know God, the more we love him.

Will Rogers once said, "I never met a man I didn't like." I always thought that statement was odd. I have met people I did not like. What he meant, I believe, is that when we get to *really* know someone, we will like him or her. This statement relates to this example of journaling. The more faithfully we keep a journal, the better we know ourselves and God. Consequently, we love God more; and our responses to that love will be to show it to others as we live our lives.

Here is a sample format of this journaling model:

Inner Introspection

Day

Complete each sentence, then circle the number that best represents your feeling of accomplishment (1 is the lowest; 10 is the highest). I have completed these sentences to illustrate my personal responses.

Today I saw God in *some friends who were helping someone else.*

Awareness of God
1 2 3 4 5 6 7 8 9 10

I felt closer to God today when _ℐ shared the listening post idea with a friend. ℐ felt God's presence._

Closeness to God
1 2 3 4 5 6 7 8 9 10

I applied God's love today in _visiting with Jack about a project. ℐ kept in mind that he, too, is God's child and treated him with more respect._

Application of God's love
1 2 3 4 5 6 7 8 9 10

Tomorrow I will allow God to _work more effectively through me as ℐ work on the new project. ℐ will listen more unselfishly to others and try to see their point of view._

MODEL TWO: Scriptural Introspection. The use of scripture as a journaling tool has long been a favorite of many. Rather than taking a cognitive approach (studying biblical background, influences, events, places, etc.), I prefer to let the scripture ask the questions for me. It is an incarnational approach—asking questions such as, "How does this apply to my life?" and, "What is my next step as it is applicable to the teachings of this passage?"

Here are passages that readily lend themselves to this kind of journaling:

Scripture	Subject
Matthew 5:3-10	Blessedness
Matthew 5:27-46	Higher righteousness
Matthew 7:24-27	Building on rock or sand
Mark 4:3-8	Parable of the sower
Mark 4:30-32	Story of the mustard seed
Luke 6:43-45	The tree and its fruits
Luke 10:30-37	The good Samaritan
Luke 12:13-21	The rich fool
Luke 15:11-32	The prodigal son
John 5:1-11	Healing
John 13:1-15	Jesus washes the disciples' feet
John 21:15-17	Loving Jesus
Romans 12:3-8	The body of Christ
1 Corinthians 12:12-27	The body of Christ
1 Corinthians 13:4-7	The way of love
Galatians 5:19-26	Fruit of the Spirit
Ephesians 6:1-18	Putting on God's armor
Philippians 3:12-16	Setting goals
Hebrews 12:1-2	Life's race

Some of the passages lend themselves to days of journaling while others may be just for one day. Regardless of which passage you choose, begin each journaling period with the following steps:

1. Quietly read the scripture and reflect on how it applies to your life.

2. Write down how you applied that scripture today.

3. Write down areas in which you need to improve.

4. Write down some ways that you can apply the teaching in the future.

Here is a sample format for this journaling model:

Scriptural Introspection
Galatians 5:19-26

Today I have shown the fruits of the Spirit by *"biting my tongue" instead of reacting poorly when the church staff noted down involving youth in the Easter service. I need to present my point of view better.*

Some areas of weakness that I have are in *HUMILITY-- It's hard for me to take a "back seat" in the overall planning.*

Tomorrow, to improve in my application of this passage, I will *focus on each person as a creation of God. I will trust his will.*

With this particular passage, you could use a page a day on each one of the fruit of the Spirit and have nine days of scriptural journaling. Also, at the beginning of each day, you could evaluate the previous day to further promote your spiritual growth.

MODEL THREE: **Prayerful Introspection.** Prayer is the primary vehicle to build bridges of communication with God. Yet, the word prayer as well as the act of prayer are often misunderstood. Writing out our prayer experiences is a form of "pragmatic prayer." We realize more fully for what we are praying and why.

A prayer journal is different than any other journal model because it is imperative that you attempt to enter all daily prayers. It necessitates taking notes of prayer thoughts and recording time and circumstances. Although that kind of busyness seems trivial, it makes dependency on God more obvious in your daily life and underscores Paul's concept of "praying without ceasing"—that is, living your life as a prayer.

For this experience, take your notebook with you wherever you go during your journaling contract. Whenever you pray, jot down the time, place, circumstance and prayer. At the end of each week, read what you have written and record on a separate page in your notebook your impressions of growth.

Prayerful Introspection

Time/Day	Place	Circumstance

Prayer _____

_____

Time/Day	Place	Circumstance

Prayer _____

_____

The following is an example of this type of journal entry:

Time/Day	Place	Circumstance
Tues. 12/3 7:15 a.m.	Bedroom	Dressing for work

Prayer *Talked to God about work today. Prayed about my meeting with Carl, and how to handle this misunderstanding of our job responsibilities. Thanked God for this new day and the potential of it.*

MODEL FOUR: **Fasting Introspection.** Fasting is one discipline that most of us avoid. We tend to be spoiled with the habit of eating three meals a day and snacking continually while watching television or sporting events. There are so many "goodies" to entice us. More than ever, we need to consider the fast as beneficial to our spiritual growth, not as a crash diet or weight loss plan. We each need to help our stomach realize that it is not our master. Anyone who ever has tried to eliminate sweets or spices from his or her diet knows that at first it is not pleasant. It seems that an insidious small voice dwells in our body saying: "Go on, eat it. You can diet later!" Do not confuse dieting with fasting. Both have different purposes. However, part of the effect of the fast is weight loss and it is usually welcome.

The purpose of the fast is to glorify God. To do this is to let God know that he is master of your life, not your stomach. It often is said, "The way to a man's heart is through his stomach." That old-fashioned notion does have a hint of wisdom for our spiritual well-being. We can, and usually do, get closer to God by becoming the masters of our stomachs. When we fast for that reason, then we become more intimate with God and more often feel his presence.

In my own experience, I have noticed that many of the hidden frustrations, angers, faults and anxieties of life have surfaced during a fast. I have been able to confront them, and in some cases, resolve them. Had I not fasted, I am relatively sure that the feelings would not have emerged. Fasting is a cleansing experience, not only of obstacles that stand between you and God, but also for your body. In a three-day or longer fast, it seems that the body compensates by adjusting fluids and waste in such a way that there is a sense of physical cleansing.

Before beginning a fast, it is important to secure permission from a physician. If the physician does not give his or her okay, then utilize another spiritual growth discipline. If the physician gives his or her okay, then proceed with care.

A person needs to get in shape for fasting much like an athlete must prepare for a game or contest. For your first fast, decide to miss one meal—preferably lunch. Lunch is generally the easiest meal to do without. When hunger strikes at noon on that day, focus on God by saying to yourself, "God is the master of my life!"

Continue to develop your fasting program by skipping lunch more often. Select a couple of days each week for a two- or three-week period.

Then you should be ready for a 24-hour fast in which you skip three meals. You are not to eat food, only drink water and other liquids. For you to get the most out of a 24-hour fast, I suggest that you decide to fast one day a week for at least three months. This schedule will give you enough time to get into a routine and let you be introspective with yourself and God.

A three- or four-day fast should be reserved for later when you have had some experience. You will find after about three days, your hunger will begin to subside. Your stomach and appetite will have adjusted, just as you will have adjusted.

Do not do an extended fast for more than four or five days without extensive study and medical supervision.

Each day that you fast, record your feelings, thoughts and insights in your journal. At the conclusion of your fasting contract, inventory your growth by reviewing your entries with an eye on what has happened to you internally—mentally and physically.

Fasting Introspection

My First Fast   Length *skipped lunch*

Date *3/18*

During this fast I felt like *my stomach ached a little but it soon passed. It didn't seem so hard.*

I thought *about how I depend on God for my health -- food and shelter -- and how much I take them for granted.*

I was surprised that *it felt so easy to do without food for a few hours.*

My Second Fast   Length *9½ hours*

Date *9/24*

During this fast I felt like *this is not really difficult. If a short fast is this good, a longer one might be better. I look forward to that!*

I thought *this is great! To be able to have uninterrupted time with God. He seems more real.*

I was surprised that *I actually look forward to this focus on God. It wasn't like waiting for Christmas, for example, but it's exciting to anticipate the next fast.*

MODEL FIVE: Study Introspection. An old farmer friend of mine reminded me that it is better to be "on the furrow instead of in the rut." He explained, "The furrow keeps on going while the rut just stays there." If we do not actively attempt new learnings, ask questions, and continually reach out to new heights of education, then we will go nowhere and wind up in a "rut." We become a candidate for burnout—regardless of our vocation.

Study of our inner self can prevent burnout. What we study tends to dictate what we are or become. As

Christians, we should study subjects and matters that are just, honorable, pure and true. In **The Celebration of Discipline**, Richard Foster discusses four steps in study.[5] He distinguishes between study and meditation and suggests that they go together—study gives structure to meditation. Any study involves four steps:

1. Repetition. I call this step "ritual." It is important to regularly channel and establish a habit of thought in a particular direction. Behavior is modified when we have a focus in a specific direction for a prolonged period. Let's face it, we are creatures of habit and that can be good.

2. Concentration. To focus and center on one subject is to increase the potential of the third step.

3. Comprehension. To comprehend is to gain valuable insight and the ability to discern.

4. Reflection. To reflect is to ask yourself, "How can what I have studied make a difference in what I am going to do with my life?"

Selecting religious books to study involves choosing to embody all the previously mentioned steps. Just reading words and being able to communicate them is not learning and growing in the faith. In order to grow personally, we must glean that which is appropriate for our lives and that which fits with who we are. We must take ownership of our faith.

Study introspection journaling is an important way to define who we are and whose we are.

Here are a few tips for choosing books and other media for study:

1. Pick a role model. Choose a Christian whom you would like to emulate. Ask him or her for suggestions of resources and study helps that have influenced his or her life.

---

[5]Richard J. Foster, **The Celebration of Discipline** (New York: Harper & Row, 1978), pp. 55-60.

2. **Go to the Bible.** Pick out areas that you are interested in pursuing because you are either intrigued or baffled and want answers. Go to the church library for reference helps. Talk with your pastor.

3. **Check denominational sources.** Ask an executive or secretary from your diocesan or conference office for a list of available study resources.

In all cases, remember the four steps of study: repetition, concentration, comprehension and reflection. Make journal entries on a regular basis. Here is a suggested model:

Study Introspection

Day *Mon., June 10*   Study Material *Book of James*

Subject *a question of faith*

My first impression of this work is *James doesn't seem to have a profound faith as Paul. He seems more concerned with works.*

The material presented makes me feel like *there may not be "one" answer to everything. I'm frustrated.*

I am having the most difficulty in comprehending — *what real belief is and how I can be sure I believe.*

Right now is a time in my life when I need to *make some significant decision about what I believe + begin living as though it's true.*

MODEL SIX: Service Introspection. To be a servant is to give up the right to be in charge. This breeds humility. In a sense, humility comes only when we do not seek it, but is a much-cherished characteristic of a Christian.

Looking inside ourselves and checking our servanthood dimension is often the first step to gaining personal Christian integrity. That is, when we realize and accept that we are not being "active" Christians, then we can plan rectifying steps. Love is a verb. It shows action. Being a servant is a visual response to God's love for us.

Service may mean that there should be projects of specific tasks that we should do, but most of all servanthood is an attitude. It is not a list of things to do, but a way of living. I already have mentioned "lifestyle Christianity." The way we show God's love is to live in the interest of others. When we do, joy tumbles forth! In fact, that is a good formula: **JOY—J**esus, first; **O**thers, second; **Y**ourself, third. When that formula is applied, there is real JOY.

Periodically look through your notebook to see if you are keeping this JOY formula intact. Then note the real joy that comes from service.

Service Introspection

Date _____9/30_____

Today I put Jesus first by _acting in the interest of someone else. I spent this Saturday morning working on Lee's old VW._

I put _Lee_ before myself today by _following through on a promise to do something with him instead of playing golf._

I am last today because _I truly did put Lee first in my thoughts and actions._

My joy today feels _pure -- there is a good feeling (and no guilt) when I do_ *as I promise. It's amazing the joy when I follow through on my word to help others.*

Has my inner life affected my outer life? *Yes!*
Explain: *My inner life seems more authentic. I no longer ask if I should do this or that. It seems natural to do the right thing.*

How has my joy affected individuals within my youth group? *Ron and Susan have talked to me about the changes in my life. They said they've noticed a change in me. I really needed that!*

Any one of the previous introspection journal models or a combination of them will give you an unbelievable insight into yourself and your relationship with God. Choose one model, follow it systematically for a block of time, then review the entries and note the changes that took place.

THE MOST DIFFICULT STEP IS THE FIRST ONE

This chapter has offered several disciplines for your own growth. The most difficult discipline for you, however, may be the discipline of managing yourself so that you get started. It is time to move on. With all the "umph" I can communicate, I urge you to choose a discipline and get started *now*! My experience is that *beginning* anything different is the most difficult part because it threatens our routine. Some people call this phenomenon "procrastination."

I was visiting with a friend recently. We were talking about effective personal disciplines. I told him about how much impact the listening post has had in my life in helping me to focus on God in everyday events. He exclaimed, "That's great! That's what I need to do!"

"When will you begin?" I asked.

My friend stammered and stuttered. He asked, "It's really hard to pin down a time, isn't it?"

I said, "Yes, it is." And that is where we left it. The last time I checked with him, he still had not started.

If you are willing to invest your time in these disciplines, you *will* grow spiritually. I encourage you to get started today.

Spiritual Growth Programs for Youth Workers

The most difficult part of a personal spiritual growth program is deciding to begin. It takes work to transform a dream or desire into a practical, meaningful program. I have been motivated many times by mountaintop retreat experiences, worship services and special programs. But often I had only foggy ideas for integrating those mountaintop experiences into my lifestyle.

Once we experience the love of God, we do not want to let it go. It is that freeing and refreshing. Have you ever been with a group of people for an extended period of time, grown close to them and not wanted to leave? Have you ever gotten so caught up in an event that you did not want it to end? Most of us have. To keep from losing that "feeling," we usually do the opposite of what we should do. We try to put a fence around those feelings by frantically buying tapes, books, and any other memorabilia that will remind us of the event and help us try to hold onto it.

The paradox of God's love is this: To have the love of God, you have to give God's love away. You must position yourself in a personal way with God to know his will for your life.

Those of us in youth ministry constantly struggle to help young people spend more time in prayer, devotions and Bible study. But we can't expect that to happen unless we ourselves are committed to a personal spiritual growth program. We must give God's love away. But first we must have it.

In this chapter, we will explore several practical programs that will help youth workers grow closer to God. These programs integrate the different spiritual growth disciplines described in the previous chapter. Before looking at these programs, let's first understand the principles that form the programs' foundations.

PRINCIPLES OF A
PERSONAL SPIRITUAL GROWTH PROGRAM

Ensure complete and fruitful spiritual growth by incorporating the following principles into your spirituality program:

1. **Private.** Your personal spiritual growth program should be a contract between you and God. It should not depend on anything else. In fact, the more discreet your program—except for its fruits—the more strength you will gain. Keeping your spiritual growth private does not mean you should deny it if asked. Rather, it means that you *live* a spiritual lifestyle, rather than talking about it. The following story illustrates the hazards of taking this privacy principle to an extreme:

A young man searching for himself joined the Marines. While waiting to report for duty, he became a new

Christian. His whole life was transformed. His parents were thrilled; they had been praying for years for him. But the young man's zeal soon worried his family. Each morning he spent an hour or more in Bible study. Each evening he kneeled beside his bed and prayed for almost an hour. During the day he proudly talked about his new spirituality to anyone who would listen.

As the time drew near for him to go into the service, his mother was worried that her son would be made fun of at boot camp. The day before he left for the Marines, his mother had a long talk with him about his new faith. She told him that when he prayed, he should do so secretly. She cautioned him to be sure to hide his Bible when he completed his daily readings and to read it only when everyone else was asleep or not around.

The eight weeks of boot camp passed and the son went home on furlough. Upon greeting his mother, he exclaimed: "You'd be proud of me! I completed eight weeks of boot camp and no one ever knew I am a Christian!"

A private spiritual growth program should not be totally hidden; however, it should not be boasted of like the Pharisees' public display of religiosity. Jesus said the attention they got was the only reward they would receive. A spiritual growth program is a sacred communication contract between you and God. People will know you are a Christian by your fruit—by your love.

2. Routine. Spiritual growth programs require personal discipline. They require consistent care and maintenance. You should have a special place and a routine for prayer and Bible study. A personal spiritual growth program must become a habit without getting "watered down" or shortened. If that happens, spiritual growth loses its power and falls into the category of "just another program."

A girl rededicated her life to God after her minister challenged the congregation to a deeper walk in faith.

She then established a discipline of prayer each night before going to bed.

When she began, her routine was to ready herself for bed, turn off the light, kneel next to her bed, fold her hands and pray aloud to God. After a few days, her knees were sore, so she changed the routine to accommodate herself. She readied herself for bed, turned off the light, got into bed and silently offered her prayers— many nights going to sleep praying. Before long even this routine became a chore. So she wrote a prayer on a poster and hung it over her bed. She readied herself for bed, turned off the light, jumped into bed, pointed to the poster and said: "There it is, God. Good night!" She then fell into a deep slumber.

This admittedly exaggerated story illustrates how we are prone to take the easy way. We often begin with great enthusiasm, but then fade out. Establish a realistic routine for your spiritual growth program, then stay with it. Do not compromise.

3. Focused. Starting a spiritual growth program without a direction or goals is like getting on your bicycle and going to the store, but not knowing what you are going to purchase. Have a specific goal in mind when beginning your spiritual pilgrimage.

Generalized spiritual goals need to be specifically fleshed out. Generalized goals are usually something like: "Be a better Christian" or "Get closer to God." Both of those are admirable and certainly important. But all of us can spend *lifetimes* reaching these goals knowing well that we can always be better Christians and get closer to God.

We need to focus the goals so that it is possible to attain them. For example, "What will it mean to be a better Christian or get closer to God?" When you have answered that, then your plan begins to take shape. Then structure your plan to move you toward your goal.

It is important to achieve your goal one step at a

time. Remember that it is a ladder with many steps. Do not try to climb to the top in one giant leap—take one step at a time. Here's a possible plan:

● Write out what you want from a spiritual growth program. For example, "I want to grow more confident in my relationship with God."

● Write out the first step you will need to take. For example, "My first step will be to establish a time each day to pray and listen to God."

● Write out when you will do the first step. For example, "I will begin next Monday at 6 a.m."

● Write out how you will follow up on yourself. For example: "I will follow up by asking myself each Monday morning how I am growing more confident in my relationship to God. After three weeks I will decide whether to continue this program, do another or take a break."

4. **Complete.** A personal spiritual growth program should be balanced. Each day should include prayer, study, faith-acting and evaluation. A shortcoming of some personal spiritual growth projects is a narrowed focus on only one area of life. It is ludicrous to pray without taking specific actions. It's pointless to study the Bible without applying its teaching at work and home. Let your whole being—mind, body and spirit— engage in your spirituality.

5. **Set limits.** The enemy of any program is having no limits. So incorporate limits as goals. For example, "For the next 30 days, I'm going to pray from 6 to 6:30 a.m. each day." Set a beginning and an end. When you have done that, not only will you have grown in your prayer life, but you also will have accomplished a goal. Your self-image grows as your self-control increases. Let me tell a story to illustrate:

My daughter (who, like most teenagers, thinks she's fat) once went on a three-day chemical diet and lost four pounds. At the end of the three days, she was more excited about the fact that she had controlled her eating habits than she was over losing the four pounds.

A spiritual growth program must have a beginning and an end. The reason some of us refrain from attempting such a project is the fear that we might be shackled to it for the rest of our lives. We know full well that we'll feel guilty if we quit. So set a limit. Begin slow and easy. Progress with caution and diligence. Then celebrate your accomplishments! When you're ready, take on another goal.

6. **Enriching.** A personal spiritual growth program enriches rather than complicates your life. The programs in this book almost always cause sighs and groans of desperation when I present them at spiritual growth seminars.

"I just don't have time to do this!"

"My schedule is full enough without adding this too."

These and similar responses indicate to me that many youth workers suffer more from poor time management than they do from anything else.

A spiritual growth program may require you to simplify your lifestyle. For example, you may need to decide to attempt a spiritual growth program instead of serving on the community youth service board. You may need to "clean out" some of the closets of your life, ridding yourself of distracting habits, beliefs and activities that you know in your heart keep you from doing first what God wants you to do. At your listening post, lay those concerns before God.

Further, a spiritual growth program should not excuse you from the essential Christian activities in your life: family life and worship.

A still painful experience from my own family life illustrates the need to enrich family life with a personal spiritual growth program. Many years ago, I had one of those everything-that-can-fail-today-did kind of days at church. I was frustrated, angry and impatient in the rush-hour traffic on the way home. When I got there, I found a house cluttered with toys, half-eaten food and other evidence of our two preschool children's presence. The smells of soiled diapers and cooking food mingled together. My wife was preparing dinner at the stove. In one arm she held our baby daughter; the other arm she used to prepare dinner. It was hot and muggy and our children were screaming. So I "rationally" greeted my wife with:

"What have you been doing all day!?"

I could have done a better job greeting my wife, of course. But I believe that had I been responsible in my spiritual life, I would have responded differently to that terrible day. First, I would have started out the day in prayer instead of panic. I would have defined a "successful" day not as one in which things go my way. A successful day is one in which I help someone in some way, regardless of my "to-do" list. I would have been aware that my family was a gift from God in spite of the stinking diapers, trashed-out house and my own bad day at the church office.

Worship in a local congregation is essential. This may seem obvious, but worship is so important that it needs to be mentioned here. During your spiritual growth program, attend at least one worship service each week. This should not be a problem. Indeed, if you do well in your program, you will eagerly anticipate worship services.

A spiritual growth program should never complicate your life. In fact, common and everyday life will be enriched by spiritual growth. But if you find your spiritual growth program taking inappropriate time or meaning from your family life and worship, stop your program and re-evaluate your schedule.

THE 30-DAY EXPERIMENT

Now put these principles into practice. Carefully fol-

low the suggested day-to-day plan so you won't miss any
ingredients. This 30-day experiment combines four disciplines that were discussed in the previous chapter:
listening post, prayer, Bible study and journaling. The
30-day experiment can be accomplished in 30 to 60 minutes per day.

FIRST DAY

---

1. Listening post (20 minutes). Get comfortable in the
area you have designated as your listening post. Kneel
on the pillow with your back straight. Open your palms
as a gesture for God to fill you. Close your eyes. Take a
deep breath as you think, "Fill me, Holy Spirit." As you
slowly exhale, say mentally, "Thank you, thank you."
Repeat this breathing exercise several times.

Next, try to imagine God; keep searching in your
mind (for however long it takes) to form an image of
God. When the image is there, you will know it. Do not
worry if this first exercise takes a long time. After the
image is clear, focus on it for as long as you can. You
may have to fine-tune it by focusing on each part of the
image and visualizing yourself with that image. Eventually, it will speak to you. Remain humble and patient
even through the distractions. Incorporate sounds or
visuals into your mental image. Allow the sights and
sounds to fade as you continue keeping God's image at
the center of your picture.

Continue listening during this time even if you do not
hear God's Word. By the end of the 30 days, you will
hear it. In each daily session, after about 20 minutes,
use your breathing exercise to allow the image to fade.
As you inhale, let the image fade; when you exhale,
mentally say, "Thank you." After the image has completely disappeared, open your eyes, get your notebook
and proceed to the journal-writing activity.

2. Journaling (10 minutes). Record your impressions

of the first 20 minutes of "listening to God." Write the most intricate details you can recall. Then in a sentence, write what you heard God saying to you. If you did not sense God speaking to you, write the most positive aspect of the 20 minutes. Record what, if any, action should come as a result of this encounter. Be specific. Following is a completed journal page:

First Day's Journal

Day *3/17*

Listening Post

My first 20 minutes were spent *in sheer agony and frustration. My mind wandered so much... thoughts difficult to control. Even focusing on outside sounds was hard.*

My image of God is *so broad, I am having trouble pinning down a specific image. I do see God holding me closely, however.*

The most positive aspect of the 20 minutes was *my realization of how independent I'm acting and how I need to focus my life on God in more specific ways.*

The specific action that must come from my encounter with God is *I need to choose one thing to focus on and concentrate all my efforts in that direction.*

I will do it *tomorrow, March 18, 6 a.m.*
(day/time)

SECOND DAY
---

1. ACTS of prayer (10 minutes). Construct a prayer list along the lines of the four-step outline in Chapter **3**. Remember the categories?

Adoration
Confession
Thanksgiving
Supplication

Develop the habit of thinking ACTS by writing your prayer the first few times. Go to your listening post and use the breathing exercises as a preliminary to constructing your list. Make a prayer list similar to the one in the following illustration:

The ACTS of Prayer

Adoration. What I most appreciate and adore about God: _____
- always there   - loves me anyway
- is comforting
- great insights into who I am

Confession. The admissions that I need to make to God—even though he already knows them: *The problem I'm having concerning acceptance of Steve. I feel he's been dishonest with me. I resent that.*

Thanksgiving. I am thankful to God for: *the peace that comes from calling on him; feeling close to him; our family's closeness; never abandoning me*

Supplication. I need God's help (and others need God's help) for: *financial problems; I need to "let go," allow God to* *lead one.*

2. Prayer (10 minutes). When your prayer list is complete, use it as an agenda for your meeting with God. Repeat the breathing exercise. As you inhale, invite God in by saying, "Come in Holy Spirit." As you exhale, tell God, "Thank you, thank you." When you have done this several times, begin your prayer: "Gracious God, I love you. I adore you . . ."

Pray for the items on your ACTS list, then conclude with this: "It is in the spirit of my Lord Jesus Christ that I say this prayer. Amen."

3. Journaling (10 minutes). In your notebook, record your experience with the ACTS of prayer. Distinguish between the words of your prayer and your images, impressions and feelings. Go into detail. It may be difficult the first few times you do it, but stick with it. The later rewards will be great. The journal page in your notebook should look similar to this:

Second Day's Journal

Date *3/18*

ACTS of Prayer

My first 10 minutes felt like *I was completing an application for a job. It was hard. I was embarrassed to write down simple things.*

When I made a list of each of the categories of the ACTS, I felt *more organized about what needed to be prayed.*

As I prayed with my list *I felt more comfortable and organized in my meeting with God—yes, it seemed that I was more prepared to pray.*

The greatest value for me today as I followed this discipline has been *I realized that prayer is serious—much of its power depends on my preparation and attitude—wow!*

The specific action that must come from my encounter with God today is *to give prayer time priority, routine and discipline. I need to talk with Steve, to tell him how I feel and ask for forgiveness.*

I will do it *March 20, before noon*
(date/time)

THIRD DAY

Every third day of this 30-day spiritual growth experiment requires an additional half-hour dedicated to Bible study. This means the Bible study time will always follow a regular listening post time or ACTS of prayer time. In the instructions for each of the 10 study days, there will be suggested scripture passages and questions for personal understanding and application.

1. **Listening post or ACTS of prayer (20 minutes).** Go to your listening post and spend 20 minutes meditating on God's Word or praying the ACTS of prayer. Then move to your study.

2. Bible study and journaling (40 minutes). Follow these Bible study instructions:

● Prepare yourself for study by using the same breathing exercise described earlier.

● Slowly read the Bible passage, savoring each word. Get used to the picture it presents. If you have difficulty concentrating on the message, read it again and again. When you have mastered what you believe to be the meaning of the passage, you are ready to commit it to memory.

● Memorize the passage. Read the first line until you sense it is time for a pause. Look up, close your eyes and say it from memory three times. As you memorize each phrase, move on to the next phrase, each time including the previous phrases all the way back to the beginning of the passage. The following is an example of how to memorize a passage.

The passage: "With so many witnesses in a great cloud on every side of us, we too, then, should throw off everything that hinders us, especially the sin that clings so easily, and keep running steadily in the race we have started. Let us not lose sight of Jesus, who leads us in our faith and brings it to perfection: for the sake of the joy which was still in the future, he endured the cross, disregarding the shamefulness of it, and from now on has taken his place at the right of God's throne" (Hebrews 12:1-2, Jerusalem Bible).

Read: "With so many witnesses in a great cloud on every side of us, . . ." Now say it from memory three times.

Continue: "We too, then, should throw off everything that hinders us, . . ." Say that from memory three times.

Now put those two phrases together. "With so many witnesses in a great cloud on every side of us, we too, then, should throw off everything that hinders us, . . ."

Now move on to the next phrase. Repeat the process until you have memorized the passage.

● In your notebook, write the passage from memory. Think about how that passage applies to you, then write that down. Give specific details about what you need to do in your life as a result of studying this passage. Write down what you are going to do and when you plan to do it. Here is a journal illustration for the third day:

Third Day's Journal

Date *3/19*

Listening Post

My first 20 minutes were spent *focusing on the word "belief." I kept letting the question, "What do you believe?" go over and over in my mind and listening for God's intervention.*

My image of God is *right now—— an all-knowing father. I sense God's presence.*

God said to me *"Don't try to answer everything right now. Take one thing at a time. Embrace it. Live it. Then move on."*

The most positive aspect of the 20 minutes was *the closeness I felt with God.*

Bible Study

For me, this passage says *that many people are watching me. I need to turn away from sin and focus on Christ. I must allow Jesus to be my life.*

During the reading of the passage, I thought and felt *a sense of community with God and other Christians. Encouragement. A sense of belonging. A sense of awe.*

The passage is as follows: "*With so many witnesses in a great cloud on every side of
us, we too, then, should throw off
everything that hinders us...*"

As I memorized this scripture, I discovered *a real
power in its meaning and an insight
of how much God loves me.*

As a result of my listening post today and my Bible
study, I need to (specific action) *surround myself
with more friends who are on the
same journey. I also need to get rid of
some selfishness by doing something
for someone else. I will take
Karen fishing.*

I will do it *by March 22, 6 p.m.*
(date/time)

POSSIBLE SCHEDULE FOR THE
REST OF THE 30-DAY EXPERIMENT

Day   Discipline
4: ACTS of prayer
5: Listening post
6: ACTS of prayer and Bible study
Scripture Passage: 1 Corinthians 13:4-7

7: Listening post
8: ACTS of prayer
9: Listening post and Bible study
Scripture Passage: Ephesians 6:18-20

10: ACTS of prayer
11: Listening post
12: ACTS of prayer and Bible study
Scripture Passage: Philippians 3:12-16

13: Listening post
14: ACTS of prayer
15: Listening post and Bible study
Scripture Passage: Galatians 5:19-26 (Memorize
verses 22-26)

16: ACTS of prayer
17: Listening post
18: ACTS of prayer and Bible study
Scripture Passage: Matthew 5:13-16

19: Listening post
20: ACTS of prayer
21: Listening post and Bible study
Scripture Passage: Matthew 7:24-27

22: ACTS of prayer
23: Listening post
24: ACTS of prayer and Bible study
Scripture Passage: Ephesians 4:22-27

25: Listening post
26: ACTS of prayer
27: Listening post and Bible study
Scripture Passage: Philippians 2:1-5 (Memorize verses
3-5)

28: ACTS of prayer
29: Listening post
30: ACTS of prayer and Bible study
Scripture Passage: Ephesians 6:1-17 (Memorize
verses 10-12, 14-17)

A variation of the 30-day experiment is to use the following formula:
Listening post: all of the odd days (1, 3, 5, etc.).
ACTS of prayer: all of the even days (2, 4, 6, etc.).
Bible study: every third day, combined with the listening post or ACTS of prayer. For your Bible study,

choose selections from Chapter 3, page 41.

After you have completed the 30-day experiment, look back over the past 30 days. What has happened to you? How has your life changed? How have you grown spiritually? After a short break, you might want to begin another experiment.

If you want to continue with another personal spiritual growth project, I suggest you look ahead to the 30 days of love, the 90-day program or even the 180-day program. Remember to give yourself a break between programs. Set parameters when you start. Do not embark on anything you will be unable to finish.

30 DAYS OF LOVE

Still another option for continuing a personal spiritual growth program is a letter-writing month called "30 days of love."

The 30 days of love program is similar to the 30-day experiment except the only discipline is writing letters. It is designed to help you contact people in your life who sometimes go unnoticed. The results of this program usually represent a change in our attitude toward others. Here is how it works:

Set a daily time and place. You may wish to use the area designated for your listening post. At the site, gather a pen, 30 envelopes, stamps, paper and a record book (the record book is not necessary, but may be used for additional exercise that I will explain at the end of this model).

Each time you write a letter, focus on one of the following daily "love words."

Love Words

Day Word	Day Word
1: Kind	4: Humble
2: Patient	5: Faithful
3: Unselfish	6: Responsible

7: Compassionate	19: Courageous
8: Trusting	20: Charitable
9: Gentle	21: Pure
10: Self-giving	22: Pure
11: Peacemaker	23: Vulnerable
12: Joyful	24: Forgiving
13: Open	25: Honest
14: Strong	26: Understanding
15: Caring	27: Sympathetic
16: Affirming	28: Empathetic
17: Truthful	29: Affectionate
18: Thankful	30: Tender

There are several ways to focus on your daily love word:

1. **Repeat the word several times.** Think about as many images of that word as you can. Think through those images and how they show love.

2. **Use a concordance.** Find as many references as you can to your daily love word.

3. **Refer to a dictionary.** Notice how many ways the love word can be used and how many different words can be made from it; for example, kind, kindness and kindly.

Begin this exercise by thinking of friends, relatives, acquaintances and contacts who in some way have touched your life. Select a person who has lived out your love word for the day. Write a "love" letter to him or her using the love word as your theme. Sign the letter. Stamp and mail it the same day.

Here's an example of a love letter. This is addressed to Vicki Stone, my sister-in-law. The day's love word is "kind."

Dear Vicki,

I just wanted to use this opportunity to tell you how much I appreciate you. Your kindness to Mom during those recent troubled times really lifted my spirits. I know you helped Mom out of a concern for her and not for yourself.

I wanted to let you know that I know about your kind deeds.

Much love,
David

Here's another example of a love letter. This one is to John Stokes, an acquaintance. The day's word is "patient."

Dear John,

You will remember me when I tell you that I was the one who kept bugging you about getting the work on my car finished by 5 p.m. on Thursday so that I could let my daughter use it to get to a meeting that night. I must have called you four or five times. You were very patient. You must have real inner strength to deal with the public in such a beautiful way.

Thank you for making my day and for giving me an example of how we should act toward each other.

Most sincerely,
J. David Stone

For each day of the 30-day period, write a letter to a different individual with that day's love word. By the time you complete the 30 days of love, you will notice that when you look at someone your thoughts and comments will be positive and loving rather than negative and ugly.

Earlier in this chapter I suggested that you use a record book for your 30 days of love project. The record book helps you keep track of your letter-writing experience.

For each letter you write, record the date, love word, name of the person, and his or her relationship to you. During the next few weeks, as you see the people you have written to, record their deportment toward you. You will be surprised at the difference your letter can make. Your record book should look similar to this:

30 Days of Love

Date	Love Word	Person	Relationship	Results
1/8	Kind	Vicki Stone	Sister-in-law	Called & said my letter lifted her spirits
1/9	Patient	John Stokes	Acquaintance	Posted my letter in his station

THE 90-DAY PROGRAM

Imagine that you've finished the 30-day experiment. You discovered the importance of ritual and, no doubt, felt a new surge in your life. Attribute the accomplishment to God. You have been experimenting with an activity that has been available all the time. You simply needed to recognize and claim it.

The 90-day program is an extension of the 30-day experiment with a few more ingredients. The 90-day program includes a listening post, prayer, Bible study and journaling, and adds unselfish acts, witnessing, letters of love and daily reports. The rationale is that we build a ritual with a number of disciplines and, at the same time, we keep our personal spiritual growth program alive, exciting and refreshing.

The following extra ingredients are for the 90-day program:

1. **Unselfish act.** During the 90-day program, one unselfish act is scheduled into each week. That is not to say this should be a rare event. You are encouraged to give many unselfish acts. By programming an unselfish act into your schedule, you will be less likely to overlook this important aspect.

An unselfish act must be exactly that—unselfish. Any act that is done with humility and without fanfare is always the best. Many times when we do something for someone else, we want accolades or recognition. You cannot be unselfish if you harbor any need for recognition.

I experienced an unselfish act early in my youth ministry career. I had just been hired as youth director for a large church—I had not met many people.

One day, the church receptionist stopped me as I passed her desk and said, "David, some lady dropped this envelope off for you." I asked who the woman was, but the receptionist said she did not know.

I opened the envelope and found two $100 bills and the following note:

David,
Please take this $200 and use it for you and your family in some fun way. Thank you for all you do for our youth.
Love in Christ,
A Christian Friend

My immediate reaction was that I needed to find the anonymous donor and return the money. Secretly, though, I appreciated the act and *really* needed the money. I asked the office staff if anyone had seen a lady come by that morning and drop off an envelope. No one had. I compared the handwriting with roll books, notes and other papers, but there was no clue as to the identity of the benefactor.

I thought that this anonymous act of giving was great, but I wondered if one really could get satisfaction through anonymous giving. Through exerience, I have found that it is satisfying to give without recognition. You do not always have to give materialistic items, you can give of yourself. In fact, some of the most meaningful gifts are when a person gives of himself or herself. Not all unselfish acts can be secret, but they are more fun if they are.

Experiment with this idea of an unselfish act before you incorporate it into the 90-day program. Think about someone who is closed up in an office or someone who is just beginning a new job. Anonymously send a flower or plant to the person. Give without acknowledgment for two reasons: so that you can watch the person's reaction and sense his or her joy, and so that you can have the experience of giving without recognition.

There are numerous service projects available in the church or community. Do not wait for project committees to ask you for help—go to them. If you wait for someone to ask you to help, you may doubt your own motives. You could think, "Oh, they caught me off guard" or "I didn't have anything else planned for Saturday afternoons." However, if you volunteer to serve, not only will you surprise the project committee, you can be more certain of your own motivation.

In the 90-day program, you will do one unselfish act a week—that is only 12 unselfish acts during the entire 90 days. Create a list of unselfish acts from which to choose. Here are some ideas:

● Find a family in need of food or clothing and begin to supply part of that need.

● Adopt a shut-in. Visit this person each week, read to him or her or help write letters.

● Volunteer your help at a community agency such as a food shelter or senior center.

● Offer to drive an elderly or handicapped person to church each Sunday.

2. **Witness.** Of course we witness our faith by the life we live, but to establish a specific discipline of witnessing as a part of the 90-day program helps to round out the total experience.

In the 90-day program, you will witness to two people a week. You will tell the people what Christ means to you and how God has entered your life.

For example, you could talk with a friend who is experiencing a letdown after recently becoming a Christian. You could help support that friend by explaining how your daily prayer life and communion with God energize you.

The most difficult type of witness is speaking up in a seemingly non-Christian environment. But it is also the most rewarding witness because of the feeling of accomplishment.

The best place to begin your witnessing discipline is with your family, not because it is easy to share with them, but because of the power that relationship will have as a result.

Years ago, Karen (my middle daughter) and I were on a trip to south Louisiana. We stopped at a general store on one of the back roads to Lake Charles. While drinking a cola and eating potato chips, we noticed cowboy hats clothespinned to a string that ran the length of the store. I tried on several hats until I finally found my size. When the clerk looked at the hat, she could not find the price tag. She looked on another hat and found it was $7.95. So that is what she charged me.

As we continued our journey, Karen wanted to try on the hat. I told her that if she would put paper inside the sweatband, it would fit her more snugly. When I turned down the sweatband, I found the price tag. It was $9.95. I commented that I had been undercharged $2.

On the return trip from Lake Charles, I once again took that old country road. Karen asked why I was going out of the way by several miles. I told her that I needed to drop the $2 off at that store.

It was several weeks after that incident that Karen asked me why I had gone to so much trouble to return the money. That was my opportunity to verbally witness to her about my faith.

For the first week of this new discipline, decide on two people to whom you will witness. During your prayer time, ask God to help you know what to say and how to say it. Follow this process throughout the program. By the end of your project, if you witness to two different people each week, you will have witnessed to 24 different people and will have established a ritual of sharing your faith.

3. **Letter of love.** Even though this discipline is in itself a program, it adds a beautiful dimension to the 90-day program. During the 90-day program, try to set aside part of one day each week for writing a letter of love (see pages 79-82).

4. **The daily report.** This is an addition to the regular journal entries that you made each day during the 30-day experiment. Each day, the first entry in your journal should be an evaluation of the previous day. The evaluation should reflect how you fared on applying your journal reflections. The following is an example of this type of journal entry:

Daily Report

Date ___6/5___

Yesterday I reflected on *how I don't spend as much time with Jeff, my son, as I need to.*

I applied the learning to my life by *inviting Jeff to ride bikes. At first he discounted the need but then agreed to go for a bicycle ride after school.*

I learned that *it doesn't take much to show attention—Jeff really seemed to enjoy the bike ride around the block. I did too!*

90-Day Program Schedule
Day Activities

1: Listening post/witness
2: ACTS of prayer/Bible study
3: Listening post/letter of love
4. ACTS of prayer/unselfish act
5: Listening post/Bible study
6: ACTS of prayer/witness
7: Listening post/worship

The above schedule runs for 90 days. Use the 30-day experiment for a model (see pages 69-79). Remember to journal each day and utilize the daily report for the beginning of each day. If the application of your journal reflections affected certain people in your life, write down the individuals' names and how they were affected. This will help you focus on these people as you proceed through your program.

THE 180-DAY PROGRAM

When you have followed a discipline as long as 90 days, it becomes a part of you. You could feel relieved when it is over; yet, you could also feel a void because something that was such a part of you is gone.

Before you start on another program, rest a few days to rebuild your hunger for communion with God. If you were faithful in fulfilling the last program, you will long for your time with God. The following story illustrates the desire of wanting to return to the Father's presence:

One wintry night when I was 10 years old, Dad told me he needed my help. We lived in a small frame house set on blocks. There was a wooden skirt around the house that usually kept the water pipes from freezing. That night was unusually cold, and my dad realized we would have to take action to protect the pipes from the cold and wind. Dad told me that we would have to wrap the pipes.

It was quite an ordeal to crawl under the house while we carried the material to wrap the pipes. The only light we had was my Cub Scout flashlight with two overused batteries. I gripped Dad's hand as we crawled through that coal-black "cave" with the small ray of light to guide us. The cold seemed to have drawn all kinds of creatures (real and imaginary). I didn't see the cat until I was about six inches away and almost put my hand on it. The cat screeched and bolted for a secret escape route. I was so terrified that I clutched Dad's hand all the more tightly. I think I temporarily cut off the circulation from his hand. I was overwhelmingly relieved that Dad was there to hold my hand.

I held the flashlight as Dad wrapped most of the pipes. My imagination and the dark began to get the better of me. I had hoped we were finished, but Dad told me there was one last chore. I would have to crawl, alone, through a narrow crawl space to the other side of the house and wrap the rest of the pipes. Dad said he would hold the light for me.

I was excited that I was going to be able to help in what seemed a very important job. The only problem was, however, I would have to crawl alone a long, long way under that dark, cold, "creature-infested" house.

I had just about finished wrapping the last pipe when the weak flashlight batteries gave out. "Turn it on! Turn it on!" I screamed. Dad tried desperately to calm me down. I was more than 25 feet away from him in complete darkness. Dad calmly guided me to him by continually talking to me and telling me to move slowly toward his voice. All the time he reassured me that there were no more creatures and that everything was going to be all right.

When I got to Dad, I grabbed him almost as firmly as he grabbed me. In his arms, my fears were totally gone. I was completely at ease and secure, for I was in my father's care. We crawled out together.

This story is similar to completing a spiritual growth program. When we finish a program, we can hardly wait to begin another one and get back into our Father's care. Begin your next big step of personal spiritual growth by trying the 180-day program.

The 180-day program is the most complete personal spiritual growth model because it includes a number of specialties that are fun and exciting. This program addresses the spiritual needs of the whole person which, when followed carefully and diligently, helps us to live a consistent Christian lifestyle.

There is a similarity of events and procedures with the other programs, but this one is more complete— wholistically and holistically. When you add a share group, Bible study group, fasting, physical exercises and a spiritual friend, you have a solid, complete program.

1. Share groups. An individual's need to belong and

be accepted by a group is paramount. Each of us has an innate need to be a part of others. Most of us do not have a strong, positive self-image.

Belonging to an authentic share group can satisfy that need to belong and it can help build a strong, positive self-image. A share group also can be called a growth group because its function is to promote an opportunity to get to know others on an intimate level in which real growth can take place. If it is true that we have a need to belong and be accepted, then our self-image is at stake.

In order that we belong to someone or to a group, we must be willing to risk ourselves. I am not suggesting that we jump off of a bridge or play Russian roulette. To risk ourselves means to open our inner life to each other. To minimize the risk, we first open up in small, authentic ways such as talking about what we like or sharing our dreams. As we share these low-risk items with others, we establish common ground. As we discover common ground, we begin to build a real friendship. The more vulnerable we are with each other, the closer we become. This concept is nothing new. It happens in all good friendships, marriages and businesses. The basic requirement to risking, however, is that we must be honest.

Structure distinguishes a share group from natural friendship-forming. With a share group, questions are usually addressed concerning each member's needs and concerns. The members are encouraged to talk about their particular hurts or the progress of their spiritual growth. Group members take turns leading the sessions. The share group is voluntary; however, it is necessary to have an unwritten contract that spells out confidentiality, attendance and accountability.

Some share groups are centered on a chosen topic. Other share groups deal solely with the needs of its members. Sometimes share groups are composed of new Christians who responded to evangelistic revivals or special meetings. Other times, share groups are formed because someone thought it would be a good idea.

For the 180-day program, you will need to be a part of one of these share groups. Ask your pastor for information about some ongoing share groups in your congregation or community. You could join one of these ongoing groups. It is difficult, however, to break into a group that already is under way because the trust level of the members may be beyond the point you are willing to go. If this is the case, you may be interested in forming your own share group.

A good way to begin a share group is to ask some of your friends if they would like to be a part of such a relationship. You will be pleased at how quickly they will agree.

Whether you join an existing group or form one yourself, remember to check these characteristics.

● **Confidentiality.** All participants must be willing to not talk outside of the group to anyone (except other group members) about what is shared in the sessions.

● **Accountability.** Each group member must be willing to be accountable to the other members as a support friend. To be accountable is to fulfill commitments and to be willing to share results and personal feelings honestly with the other members.

● **Attendance.** All groups must set parameters such as the meeting time limit and the number of sessions. Choose a time which will be suitable for all participants; for example, "We will meet from 6 to 7 a.m. each Thursday from January 4 to March 2." A minimum of a dozen sessions is suggested. The ideal size of the group is five to eight members, but never more than 12. The smaller the group, the better the atmosphere for sharing.

● **Non-judgmental.** Each member should pledge to be

supportive and affirming and *not* use judgmental language; for example, "You shouldn't have done that" or, "I can't believe you said that."

A share group functions best when it meets in the homes of its members. Establish a rotation system for the meetings, then prepare a calendar for each member which states the dates, times and addresses.

Here are several possibilities for subject material:

● Each member is responsible to prepare a "thought-for-the-week." It is not to last more than five minutes. Use that thought for a springboard into the rest of your meeting.

● Your group may be compiled of people who have decided to do the 180-day spiritual growth program, or your group may be an extention of a Sunday school class, or your group may have come together with a common need to draw deeper in faith. Utilize the diverse backgrounds of your participants and ask them for ideas they would like the group to discuss. You also can check with your pastor or church library for material.

2. Bible study group. For 90 days of the 180-day program, you should belong to a Bible study group. This group may be made up of the same people in the share group.

Because of its nature, the Bible study group should be structured more tightly than the share group. At the outset, decide on parameters—a definite beginning and end. The group should be kept small and personal. In addition, regular attendance should be stressed, if not contracted. Choose from scores of Bible study materials after consulting with your pastor.

3. Fasting. For the fasting model in your 180-day program, you will fast only one day a week. I suggest that you begin the program by deciding to fast only one meal at first. Then after several weeks, increase to the 24-hour fast (see Chapter 3). Journaling your experiences will aid you in evaluating and charting your growth.

4. Physical exercise. In any wholistic program of growth, you should include physical exercise. This can be either structured through a health club or in your own personal discipline.

A routine of physical fitness three days a week during the 180-day program adds a significant integration of the mind, body and spirit.

It is no secret that when you are rested, you function better in your thinking capacity and your emotional responses to those around you. Just as you need to keep your mind alert and your emotions in check, you need to keep your body fit. When stress comes, it affects the body, too. If you are in shape, you can handle stress better.

Before you begin an exercise program, seek advice from a physician or professional at a local health club. Ask your friends what they do for physical exercise, then apply some of their suggestions to your program.

5. Spiritual friend. A spiritual friend will not force you to do all of your spiritual disciplines, but he or she will serve as a guide to keep you honest during the 180-day personal spiritual growth program. After selecting your spiritual friend, meet with him or her at least two times during your program (see Chapter 3).

Wholistic and holistic personal spiritual growth embodies four areas: spiritual, physical, mental and emotional.

The premise is that we must develop each of these areas to have a balanced life. Only an extended period such as the 180-day personal spiritual growth program can offer total maintenance and growth for an individual.

It's important to follow through on decisions and resolutions that are made in spiritual growth programs. I assure you that if journaling (or any discipline) becomes perfunctory, you will become bored, disenchanted, distressed and finally depressed. You will be worse off spiritually than before you began the program. On the the other hand, if you allow the program to work in your life, you will feel not only a sense of satisfaction but notice how life around you seems to take on a more significant meaning. Your awareness level of people, places and events will change. Your spiritual growth will emerge and show itself by your response to your environment. You will love yourself more. You will love others more and God will become more real.

PART THREE

SPIRITUAL GROWTH FOR YOUTH GROUPS

Caring

Spiritual growth must be the first priority in a complete youth ministry program. Every retreat, program, party or project needs to be planned with spiritual growth in mind. The group needs to grow as individuals and as a whole.

When youth groups fail, we usually pin the reason for failure on the weather, the minister, the "bad counselors," the "phase" the youth are going through or some other excuse. Most often, however, it is a lack of spiritual growth as top priority. How many times have you heard people say they have "burned out"? They usually quit their job and go into another field, seek a new job in the church or go back to school. My hunch is they are not burned out; they have lost God. They feel the God who called them originally is not present with them now. They have lost contact by allowing other matters to take God's place. We cannot count on other matters to take the place of God. The same is true of a youth group. We know there is a problem when statistics show that two of 10 youth who regularly attend church do not even know why Easter is celebrated. By focusing too much on trips, ski retreats and attendance, we lose the whole notion of why we are coming together. Programs, activities and recreation are important and have their place in youth work. A sense of spirituality must permeate throughout them all.

We need to remember that relationships are absolutely crucial to spiritual growth in youth groups. Did a program bring you to Christ? No. You are a Christian because of a person. A person helped you grow. And your relationships with young people and adults involved in youth work will prove the most important factor in youth ministry spiritual growth.

As you read the following chapters, keep in mind that the common thread that binds these models and programs is the quality of relationships. Also keep in mind that your most important relationship is with God. If you skipped the previous chapters in order to get to youth group programs—stop. Go back and read them. Remember: You can't give away something you don't have. Spiritual growth begins with you. Work first on your relationship with God—only then will the programs provide authentic ministry for young people.

Now let us look at our youth group. The second chapter highlighted the findings of George Gallup Jr. and David Poling that we need to "... get used to a new word: spirituality."[1] The second chapter also shared Merton Strommen's findings that "... three out of four want to be a part of a caring, accepting group."[2]

On the basis of these findings, our youth groups must provide an environment of acceptance and belonging that focuses on spirituality. We must have ministry of not only friendship with each other, but first with God.

[1]George Gallup Jr. and David Poling, **The Search for America's Faith** (Nashville: Abingdon, 1980), p. 34.

[2]Merton P. Strommen, **Five Cries of Youth** (New York: Harper and Row, 1979), p. 27.

In this chapter we will explore the possibilities for caring for one another as brothers and sisters in Christ.

We are creatures of habit. Most of us get up at a certain time in the morning. We usually eat three meals a day whether we need them or not. We follow established routines each day from plugging in the coffee pot in the morning to turning the light out after the nightly news broadcast. When that routine is interrupted, we tend to be grouchy, irritable and plain hard to get along with. Our security has been tampered with.

When we feel secure, we are more able to make choices, get along socially, and not worry unnecessarily about the day's unmet goals and frustrated expectations. Spirituality needs to be ritualistic and a part of everything in a youth group. An attitude of God's love must prevail in every activity, relationship, song and prayer. Let's look at the caring rituals of the "ring-up," sharing of joys and sorrows, comfort and sharing, and what I call an ICU (intensive care unit).

THE "RING-UP"

One of the simplest rituals of caring that we have traditionally used in our youth group is the ring-up. At the beginning of every youth meeting, we gather in a circle, put our arms around each other, welcome everyone and have an opening prayer. This experience enables the actives, inactives and friends of the youth group to feel a sense of belonging to a family. Ring-up serves as a "get together and let's get started" time. We also use ring-up to give instructions for the program.

You may be thinking about using ring-up with your own group right now, but you have some reservations about your kids touching each other. Most self-conscious young people cannot bring themselves to touch someone because they do not know the person or are afraid of being rejected. Young people love to touch, and what's more, they are doing it. We need to teach them how to do it appropriately.

For example, try not to come on too strong with your kids. I am a hugger. I am warm, sensitive and love to be there for kids. Maybe you are that way, too. A long time ago, I read that youth need to be hugged. I already knew that! I had been doing it for years, but never really thought that it was all that important. I remember my first Sunday gathering as a youth director at another church. I was waiting at the double doors when the first two youth showed up. I had met one of the girls briefly before, but I had never seen the other. I rushed to them, threw my arms around each one, gave them a big hug and exclaimed I was glad to see them. I noticed that they backed off a little. I continued in that manner to greet everyone who came. I later learned from one of the youth that my initial "hugging" was a little much. He told me that people thought I was weird. Some even thought I was a dirty old man! That hurt my ego. My intentions were pure; however, I scared some people off by my gregarious nature and insensitivity to their feelings. Now, rather than do away with hugs, I just do not come on so strong. I try to remember that youth really want to be touched, but it must not be thrust on them.

In the ring-up, sometimes there are those who self-consciously lag back and do not feel comfortable putting their arms around their neighbors. Do not insist by saying, "Come on, come on, nobody is going to hurt you." So many times we say that kind of thing in a situation because we feel we must have the perfect project or, in this case, the perfect circle. More harm than good may be done if we insist.

One way to help involve everyone in the ring-up is to secretly recruit a few outgoing, popular kids to be on the lookout for those who are lagging back.

I call the recruits the S.S.S. (Stone's Secret Service). I

talk with the recruits about the dynamics of the ring-up
and teach them how to sensitively involve those self-
conscious kids. I ask the S.S.S. to watch for those cases
and move between them to complete the circle. The
S.S.S. helps overcome the early resistance to the ring-
up.

Make the ring-up a ritual for the beginning and close
of each meeting. It will not be long before everyone not
only expects the ring-up, but looks forward to it.

We often use the ring-up before we go on a trip.
Many times we incorporate the pastor and the parents
who are at the bus to say goodbye. With parents, youth,
friends and pastor all circled together, we ask God for
blessings and safety for our trip. When we return we
repeat the same ritual.

As we belong to one another in Christian fellowship,
we belong to God. That is why the ring-up is essential in
our group. It not only satisfies "skin hunger" but is the
preamble of a deeper walk and trust in Christ.

SHARING OF JOYS AND SORROWS

Another ritual of caring is the sharing of joys and
sorrows. As you begin this model, tell your youth group
that each meeting will have a time set aside for the
sharing of joys and sorrows. Explain that when we
share with one another our joys and sorrows and pray
to God, we build a loving Christian family.

Ask the group members to think about the joys they
have to celebrate and the sorrows for which they need
guidance or support. Tell the youth that as they share
their joys and sorrows, you will list them on a tablet.
After the youth have shared, you will lift the petitions
to God in prayer. You go first! Tell the group about a
joy or sorrow you have such as: "I have a joy. My
daughter just got a job and is excited." Write it down
on your pad. Now ask the group if there is anyone who
would like to share a joy or sorrow. Give the young peo-

ple time and give them some examples such as: "Do you have a relative who is facing surgery?" Or, " Do you have friends who are facing touch decisions?" Or, "Do you have any successes or accomplishments for which you are thankful?"

As you write down the prayer requests, attempt to personalize them. Ask questions such as: "What is your grandmother's name?" Or, "Would your friend mind if we used her name in our prayer?"

Allow several minutes for the total group to share, then ask the youth to join hands and bow their heads. Use the list of suggestions and begin praying:

"Gracious God. We love you. We believe in you. We come to you in prayer this evening sharing our joys and our sorrows. George's grandmother, Jenny, is facing surgery on Tuesday. We ask that you give her comfort and surround her with your love and peace. Be with the physician who attends her and all others who nurse her back to health."

At the conclusion of each petition, have the group join you in saying. "Oh Lord, this is our prayer." This affirmation will strengthen the bonds of friendship and community as well as help each individual focus on the specific petitions.

The first time you attempt this sharing, there will probably be some hesitation to volunteer joys and sorrows. Remember that you have asked people to share something important. As they reflect on the relationships and needs in their lives, they need time. So pause long enough to allow them to think and then speak. It takes time to build up a trust level in which the youth believe that this is really what you want them to do and that their requests are acceptable by you. Before authentic sharing can or will occur, the youth must feel comfortable and secure with you and feel that they can count on you.

After several weeks of leading sharing of joys and

sorrows, hand off leadership to the youth. When this time comes, ask the youth to make small circles of five or six people. For a greater feeling of security, have each cluster of youth pull their chairs close together. Invite someone from each group to be the chaplain and hand each of them a sheet of paper and pencil. Ask each chaplain to lead a four- to five-minute discussion and list the joys and sorrows on the paper. Then, ask the chaplains to lead their groups in prayer using the items on their lists as prayer petitions. Ask the groups to hold hands or put their arms around each other. Give instructions that when the groups finish, they may talk quietly until the others have completed their prayer time. Conclude with a large group prayer or song.

If you are diligent with this ritual, you will find that real depth will begin to emerge in your group and an attitude of togetherness will prevail. The youth will look forward to this time of prayer more than anything else that your church can provide—including parties, programs, retreats and trips.

THE RITUAL OF COMFORT AND CARING

Comfort and caring is designed to augment the sharing of joys and sorrows on retreats and youth group meetings away from the church. Comfort and caring is based on physical needs that require immediate attention. They are usually practical things such as: "I left my sleeping bag." Or, "I didn't bring any toothpaste." Everyone has a chance to voice a need and the total group has a chance to respond. Comfort and caring operates on the principle that there is someone in the group who can meet almost any need that might arise.

Years ago, before my youth group knew about comfort and caring, we went on a retreat. During that time, one of the boys never went swimming. When asked why, he said, "I don't want to." We later found out that he had wanted to go swimming, but had forgotten his swimsuit and nobody in his cabin had an extra. If we had only known about comfort and caring, he could have gone swimming—one of the boys in another cabin had brought two suits.

Most youth feel happy to assist someone and will often sacrifice their only other towel just to help out. Comfort and caring helps to build a compassionate youth ministry.

Recently at a retreat in south Louisiana, we took time out for comfort and caring. One girl said that while she was coming from her cabin that night to the fellowship hall, she lost her glasses. She was afraid someone would accidentally step on them and smash them. As a result of comfort and caring, we put together a flashlight brigade during the break time and went on a search. The glasses were found and a damsel in distress was saved. The villain (not caring) was defeated. Thank you, hero (comfort and caring).

THE ICU (INTENSIVE CARE UNIT)

George Gallup Jr. found that nearly half of the surveyed youth would respond if they were asked to help in Sunday school, Christian education, youth activities, social work, church music, sports programs and fellowship events.[3]

It is important for you, the leader, to keep this fact in mind as you work in youth ministry. Most youth will volunteer if they are simply asked.

The Intensive Care Unit is one method of caring for and being aware of the needs of the youth group. The ICU is made up of a team of youth who have volunteered or have been recruited by the youth leader.

Just as a hospital has an intensive care unit for its patients, so can the youth group. The purpose of a hospital's intensive care unit is to monitor patients meticu-

---

[3]Gallup and Poling, **The Search of America's Faith**, p. 24.

lously to prevent the deterioration or spread of a dangerous situation. It is personal care. Often it is more than one-on-one. It utilizes the skills of many and calls in specialists when necessary.

The youth group ICU functions the same way: keeping and checking attendance, carefully watching for any problems that may arise, caring for all youth group members, and calling in a specialist (minister, youth director, counselor or teacher) when there is a problem the ICU cannot handle. The ICU is a sensitive, caring, and action-oriented group that must keep certain matters confidential and not fall into the trap of gossip.

When you first begin an ICU with your youth group, explain the concept and duties of the program. Mention that within two weeks you will be selecting the first unit. After a four-week training period, the program will begin. Suggest that those who would particularly like to be a part of the ICU to contact you during the week. This process allows for those who really feel a compassionate urge to help others to step forward. Find a spot for anyone who signs up—turn no one down.

Select four to six youth for the ICU. A small group is important when you begin because of the personal and confidential nature of the group. Later on, when you have handed over the leadership responsibility somewhat, a ratio of one ICU member to every 12 members in the group is appropriate.

After you have selected members for the ICU, plan four two-hour training sessions and prepare an agenda. Mail the agenda along with a letter to each member. Following are examples of a letter and agenda.

Dear Susan,

I am so pleased to welcome you to First Church's youth ministry Intensive Care Unit. Your selection for this servant opportunity means that I believe you to be a sensitive, caring and ready-to-work member.

Our youth group includes active members, inactive members and their friends. In the Intensive Care Unit, we will have the awesome responsibility to do things such as keep attendance, learn to recognize the needs of each individual and formulate plans to "be there" for one another.

Susan, I am so excited about this part of our ministry. I believe that it is at the heart of what Christianity is all about—touching people where they hurt even as Christ did and does through us.

I am enclosing the agenda for the ICU training program. Notice that we only have four two-hour sessions. That means they will be packed with learning modules so that we can do the very best job possible. Mark the dates on your calendar. All ICU members must be present for all sessions.

Again, congratulations on your selection as an ICU member. I am looking forward to getting to know you better and serving our young people with you.

In Him, we really are one.

Agenda for ICU Training
(Post this agenda in a prominent place!)

All four training sessions will be conducted on Tuesday nights from 7 to 9 p.m. Bring your Bible.

SESSION ONE
Tuesday, September 10
David Stone's home
200 Medallion Circle
636-9012

- Orientation/review agenda/covenant statement
- Servanthood concept (Philippians 2:19-30)
- Discussion of the overall program
- Refreshments and ring-up

SESSION TWO
Tuesday, September 17
Susan O'Neal's home
1244 E. Lynn Avenue
861-0115

- Bible study (1 Corinthians 12:12-27)
- Record keeping: role books, registration, contacts, referrals, follow-up cards, phone calls and visits
- Refreshments and prayer

SESSION THREE
Tuesday, September 24
Bobby Bell's home
1200 Fairfield, Apt. 206
869-3188

- Bible study (Luke 10:30-37)
- Identify needs/form a plan/role play
- Refreshments

SESSION FOUR
Tuesday, October 1
Linda Snyder's home
1160 Wildwood
868-6006

- Bible study (Ephesians 6:1-18 and Philippians 3:12-16)
- Review
- Case studies on referral
- Assignments
- Refreshments

All ICU training sessions should begin with a Bible study on the concept of servanthood. An easy way to find scripture references on this topic is to check the concordance of your Bible. Some examples are: Matthew 23:11-12; Mark 9:35; 10:43-44; Luke 22:26-27; John 12:26.

Regularly schedule a two-hour period for all of the meetings. It is important to keep these sessions informal. Meeting at various homes and serving refreshments help to keep them that way.

Following are more details on each of the four ICU training sessions:

Session one. At the beginning of the orientation meeting, review the entire agenda which outlines the course. After the members have an idea of what the ICU program entails, ask them to sign a covenant statement such as:

```
┌─────────────────────────────────────────┐
│                                         │
│   I will attend all training sessions   │
│   for the Intensive Care Unit.          │
│                                         │
│                                         │
│   _____   │
│            (Signature)                  │
│                                         │
└─────────────────────────────────────────┘
```

Help the youth get the "feel" of what their mission will be in the ICU. One way to do this is to use a scripture as the basis of the mission. For example, discuss Paul's concern for the Christians he nurtured and loved (Philippians 2:19-30). You also could compare the mission of the ICU to the servanthood concept of Jesus, "If any one would be first, he must be last of all and servant of all" (Mark 9:35). Another way of relating the mission of the ICU is to discuss the acronym JOY: Christians are to focus on Jesus first; Others second; Yourself third.

When you have had a chance to share the biblical concept and rationale for the ICU, give each member a copy of the following responsibilities:

● Performing a weekly "checkup" of every youth on the actives, inactives and friends lists.

● Formulate a plan of discovery and action for any youth in need.

● Make assignments for the action and carrying it out.

● Refer difficult concerns to the proper people (pastor, youth director, counselor or teacher).

Be sure to say this is a list of responsibilities and is only a starting place; any one of the points may be negotiated, dropped or added to. This will give your new ICU a sense of authenticity and let them know that you not only are willing to share the responsibility of the intensive care of the youth group, but *expect* to share it with the ICU members.

Give each person a chance to express how he or she feels about the concept of ICU. Sit in a circle and ask each person to complete the sentence, "I accepted the volunteer position in ICU because . . ." You begin and then proceed around the circle. Go around the circle three times. You will be amazed at the amount of personal information that will emerge and also at how uniform the conceptual thinking will be. Circle-sentence sharing has the unique characteristic of consolidating ideas, concepts, and commitments and forming them into a single purpose.

The entire two hours need not be spent in intensive sharing. Remember this is informal. Include refreshments and a ring-up prayer to close the session. Be sure you do not go over the two-hour limit.

Session two. Allow 30 minutes for you to lead the Bible study and give a brief explanation of the night's agenda. Use circle-sentence sharing to personalize and crystalize the scripture passage. Form a circle and ask each youth to complete the following sentence, "To me, this Bible passage means . . ."

Explain the ICU task of record keeping—the mechanical aspects and importance of keeping attendance records for each member of the youth group.

Keeping attendance seems so bureaucratic and mundane. Most of us resist it because it seems so foreign to "ministry." Yet, if we can develop an understanding that each number represents a person, our task will be much more personal and take on a greater significance.

As a large group, brainstorm for new ways to design the roll books and get new participants each week. Discuss ways of activating the inactives and keeping in close touch with the actives. Talk about possible methods of responding to friends of the youth group.

One example of increasing attendance is to plan a weekly contest similar to "guess the number of marbles in the fishbowl." Design a registration card for everyone to complete. The card should have spaces for the participants to fill in their name, phone number and guess. If one does not sign up, he or she will not have a chance to win the prize. Prizes can include free pizza, movie tickets, skating rink passes and golf course discounts. Many businesses offer these prizes free of charge in order to promote themselves.

Ask the ICU members to help you develop a sensitive plan of follow-up on absences. One of the reasons people become members of an organization or group is they have formed a habit of attendance. The reverse is also true. "Staying away" becomes a habit and the longer people stay away, it's less likely they will return.

One way to follow up on absences is, when a person misses one time, send a card just to let the person know you missed him or her. If the person misses two times in a row, give him or her a phone call. Do not ask: "Where were you?" Or, "Where have you been?" Make a statement of a more caring nature such as: "We missed you at youth group. I am just calling to check on you. Is there anything I can do to help?" Most contacts like these are warmly received and bring results of the missing member returning to youth group. It is difficult for a person to return to a group if he or she has been away a long time. Youth with a poor self-image feel as though they will not be accepted. A personal call on the phone is a boost and an important part of the Intensive Care Unit.

If someone has been absent for as much as three weeks in a row and does not respond positively to the phone call during the second week, a home visit is in order. Each individual situation must be analyzed before you determine who makes the visit.

For those who are only involved in the youth group as friends of youth group members, creative ways of keeping contacts become a challenge, but reap a lot of rewards.

Close the second session by asking the members to share the most significant thing that they have learned. This will cement some of the points made and serve as an evaluation. Close with prayer and enjoy the refreshments.

Session three. For the Bible study, choose a parable such as the good Samaritan or a scripture revolving around Jesus' ministry to the sick. After reading, studying and discussing the passage, ask the youth how they could apply the message to the youth group.

Ask the members to list individual and group needs. Individual needs could include: going into the hospital for a tonsillectomy, getting wisdom teeth pulled, being ill, being involved in an accident or having trouble within the family. Group needs could include: growing number of inactives or low participation in discussion.

Discuss each need in detail and talk about what action should take place and by whom. The action may involve a visit, prayer, phone call or letter. Very often, referral is the action for a delicate situation. Tell the youth that they will discuss referrals at the next training session.

When you have completed the necessary discussion, role play some of the situations and the suggested actions. Ask the youth if their plans seem to work according to the role plays. Are there some actions that need to be altered? kept the same? Formulate a definite plan of action for the presented needs.

Close with prayer and refreshments.

Session four. The final session is a review of ICU, a lesson on communication and assignments. Following the Bible study and discussion, ask someone to volunteer to give a review of what ICU is all about. Lead a discussion on what has been learned up until the present. Ask questions such as: "What is the lesson that most stands out in your mind?" "How will you apply ICU training to your life?"

Give a quick review of the previous session. Ask the youth how they know which situations they can handle and which they would need to refer. Give the following guidelines: "If you ever feel that a situation is something we should not handle or if you feel uncomfortable about it, there is a possible need to refer. It also is important to remember that people in delicate situations need our help in ministry. There is no need for us to gossip to others about the situations."

Give the young people some examples of referral situations such as pregnancy, suicide threats or alcoholism. The following is an example of a decision to refer:

When the word was out that Lesley was pregnant and was afraid to tell her family, our ICU group did not want to "rat" on her, yet felt that she needed to talk to someone who could help her. It was decided that someone would talk to her best friend (who was not a member of the youth group) about it. The plan was to get her best friend to suggest that Lesley talk with her youth director. I was that youth director. I have found when people ask you for help, they are more open to your counsel than if you offer to help without their asking. Through the relationship I had with Lesley and her family, I was able to minister to her. The ICU had met a need and implemented a successful plan of action.

Assignment time is an integral part of the last training sessions. By this time, you will have a chance to evaluate each ICU member's special interests and abilities.

List all of the possible tasks and make the initial assignments. Explain your rationale, and tell the members that they are responsible for tasks now listed and new ones that develop. Explain that a rotation assignment will be in effect. Each person will, at some time, have an opportunity to serve in each responsibility. Some of the beginning tasks might be:

- Making up the attendance roll
- Marking or recording the weekly attendance
- Making weekly announcements concerning needs of youth
- Hosting weekly ICU meetings
- Establishing the referral liaisons and relationships

After the training sessions, ICU will continue to meet weekly. These weekly meetings will help all ICU members to be aware of the condition of the youth group. Each meeting should include the following steps:

- Bible study
- Discussion of past week
- Discussion of problems, needs, or ways to involve actives, inactives and friends
- Forming a plan of action
- Making assignments
- Refreshments and prayer

At one of our ICU meetings, we spent some time talking about the guests of the past week. Brenda observed that one guest was on the newspaper staff at school. She suggested that the ICU ask him to help out with the youth group newsletter.

Discussing how to involve guests will create an

awareness of new members and build a sensitivity toward them. The following story illustrates this point:

Susan's friend Debbie came to youth group one night. Debbie was not a physically attractive girl and seemed very much into herself. Our youth group was nice to her at first, but when she did not respond positively, she was ignored. My thoughts were to admonish the group for not being Christian. Fortunately, I held back until I got to the ICU meeting that week. After discussing actives and inactives, I was astounded when Richard said, "We need to discuss Debbie." I sat back and let this "seasoned" ICU member work out the problem. The pleasure derived from watching and listening to those youth form a workable solution to the situation was wonderful and worth every effort to plan and train them.

Richard began by telling the group he had noticed how cold our group had been to Debbie and how it must have made her feel, not to mention how Susan, our youth group member, must have felt. He recounted some statistical data that he had heard in one of our training sessions. "Many people with a poor self-image hide inside themselves and often present a negative attitude," he said.

Barbara confirmed what he had said and asked, "As a Christian fellowship, what can we do?" An excellent discussion followed, peppered with scripture, Christian principles and personal testimonies. It was finally decided that Barbara would visit with Susan, tell her of our discussion and make plans with Susan to bring Debbie again. Each member of the ICU was to be on the alert when Debbie came back and make a special effort to engage her in conversation, make sure there were no put-downs and involve her in some way. All of that conversation took place without my input at all. I could not believe it—ICU was working!

When Sunday evening came and Debbie walked in

with Susan, it was like "old home week." Debbie eventually joined the youth group and became a vital part. And you know what? Debbie is married now, has a baby and is serving as chairperson for the church membership care program. I wonder how that ever came about?

With each year's fellowship, there will be significant differences in the ICU simply because personalities differ and youth groups differ. But the needs are there and the youth are there to meet those needs. Take a calculated risk, let them minister. Your whole group will benefit because the young people will be helping. Remember they want to help!

6

Bible Study

Jeff, First Church's fledgling youth director, was a new Christian. He was a model of youth and vigor. As an excited, exuberant and "hip" Christian, Jeff used his first meeting to tell the group of his struggle with drugs and stealing and how he had turned his life over to the Lord. Everyone was impressed. He was authentic and sincere. Then he told the youth group members that while they were yet sinners, God loved them and wanted them to study the Bible to make the same discoveries he had. Jeff announced the formation of a midweek Bible study group that he would lead. The study would go for as many weeks as "the Lord allowed."

Throughout the next several months, the Bible study grew and a number of youth came to know Jesus. But many others "fell by the wayside." When Jeff was asked why more youth did not participate, he responded, "Many are called, only a few answer" and he quoted a scripture reference.

Let's look at Jeff's approach to Bible study.

The youth director had a relationship with God. *Good.*

He was authentic and sincere. *Good.*

He taught the Bible study. *Good.*

He assumed what God wanted for the youth group members. *Bad.*

The Bible study was conducted regularly on Wednesday nights. *Good.*

Many youth came to Jesus. *Good.*

Many youth "fell by the wayside." *Bad.*

Jeff failed to give a proper answer about the number of participants. *Bad.*

The Bible study went on indefinitely. *Bad.*

Jeff did many right things, but in the wrong way, or for the wrong reason or in the wrong place.

Bible study is one of the more misused and poorly led activities among youth groups. A major study by the Gallup organization points out a myriad of problems:

> *A most disturbing finding is an epidemic of ignorance about the most basic Bible content. Youth simply don't know the Bible (although chances are high that most adults are also bibically illiterate). For example, only 35 percent can name five or more of the Ten Commandments and only three in 100 can name all 10. Twenty percent of those who regularly attend church worship services do not know why Easter is celebrated. One-half of regular church attenders can't name the titles of the four Gospels. Two out of 10 regular church attenders don't know the correct number of Jesus' apostles.*
>
> *These findings are even more disturbing since Gallup also found that four in 10 teenagers are involved in some kind of Bible study group. A similar number of teenagers read their Bibles at least weekly. With Bible ignorance so rampant, one won-*

ders: *What is being taught at these Bible study groups?*[1]

Reread the last sentence of the quoted material. One major reason I believe Bible studies are often "less than effective" is the lack of authentic purpose. Bible study should provide a setting for relational spiritual growth. If we work on relationships first, the Bible's content will be remembered as youth incorporate it into their lifestyle.

We should consider who young people are, their needs, and their desire to belong and be accepted. We are vehicles for God. We must, by example, be there for youth and share with them what God has done in our lives. We need not lecture. In the above illustration, the youth director created in "his" Bible study more "little Jeffs" rather than challenging each participant to be a follower and believer in his or her own right.

Bible study must harmonize with faith formation. Some youth are not yet ready for Bible study. But many are. So Bible study should be encouraged but not required from a young person in order to be in youth group. Jeff might have better led the Bible study by placing young persons' needs before his own. Rather than telling them what decisions to make, Jeff could have helped the youth build a faith foundation of their own for when he no longer was there.

IN THE BEGINNING ... SHARING YOUR STORY

Sharing your personal story to the entire youth group is an excellent way to begin. Talk about how Bible study is important to you right now, not in the past. Talk about what you have learned and how you have applied it to your life. Explain that you are not perfect and need God's revelation each day to grow. Share that

---

[1]"Religion in American Research," GROUP Magazine (November/December 1984): 27.

the Bible (God's Word) is a collection of humanity's encounters with God. Tell the youth that the power and wisdom that was available in biblical times is available to us, too. As we explore and try out for ourselves these timeless truths, some will fit and others will not at this particular time. One thing is for sure, God will speak to us through his Word.

As you explain how everyone is at a different place in his or her spiritual growth, invite the youth to contract for a specific period of time (for example, one hour a week for 13 weeks) to meet, study and share in a Bible study.

THE FIRST MEETING

"Informal" and "optional" are necesasry characteristics of a good Bible study group. The kind of Bible study I am suggesting is not "systematic" such as Sunday morning church school, but an informal group study. Informality is important so that nobody feels pressure to belong. Informality also helps establish some initial common ground for participants. Those who come want to be there and the contract is clear: The participants are there to study the Bible.

In the initial meeting, I like to give all present an opportunity to explain why they came and discuss what they hope to accomplish. I always go first and then give each one a chance to explain. I let everyone know that it is okay to pass.

It is important to establish common ground, but it is also important to have some "meat" in the meeting. Many study groups fail because they omit the "meat"; however, many groups fail because "meat" is all they offer. As with everything, balance is key.

THE FIRST SEVERAL MEETINGS

Always begin each of the first meetings with a non-threatening exercise or conversation starter. For example, split the young people into small groups of three or four people each. Then ask them to complete conversation-starting sentences such as:

"My most exciting moment was . . ."

"My favorite room in the house is . . ."

"My favorite vacation was . . ."

"If I had one wish that would come true, it would be . . ."

This type of open-ended sentence is very helpful in establishing common ground. Once common ground is established, it is much easier for people to share more deeply. Unless common ground is established, asking people what Bible passages mean to them will tend to cause nervous and less-than-authentic responses.

Establishing common ground is especially important the first few meetings when the participants are getting to know each other. The comfort level will increase with each meeting. Gradually add more study material and in-depth sharing. Eventually, the youth will open up as they feel more secure that they will be accepted. They want spiritual nourishment, but not at the expense of being embarrassed.

THE LAST SEVERAL MEETINGS

The last six or seven meetings should focus on deeper sharing. The accountability factor will give plenty of impetus for that. Each meeting will still be opened with a time for the participants to "unpack their bags" with each other, but the time allotted for that decreases with each meeting. The allotment of time for establishing common ground looks something like this:

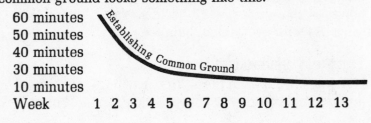

EVALUATION

Evaluation will be the most exciting part of the entire 13-week study. Some groups plan a meal to celebrate the time spent learning together. Others simply meet one more time in a free-for-all sharing session in which each person talks about his or her own growth. Another valuable method is individual evaluation. The leader meets with each participant, one-on-one, and talks about his or her growth and credos. This sit-down discussion is often the beginning of a spiritual friend relationship.

A BIBLE STUDY MODEL (13 WEEKS)

Preparation

1. **Design a contract.** Include the following covenants:
- I will attend all 13 weeks of Bible study.
- I will read my weekly assignment.
- I will refrain from all "put-downs" during the Bible study meeting.
- Any change in this contract will be negotiated with the group.
- Whatever I decide to do as a response to the Bible study, I will be accountable to the group for carrying out my decision.
- I will write two credos: one before and one after the Bible study. Upon completion of the Bible study, I will discuss the credos with the Bible study leader.

2. **Decide on a place and time of meeting.** You must be consistent with the time. The place can be negotiated. To keep the Bible studies informal, it is best to meet in the leader's home or the home of one of the members. (Let the students volunteer their homes.) Always ask someone to volunteer to furnish refreshments for the close of a session.

3. **Prepare the materials and assignments.** I know it is a hassle to make preparation for the entire 13-week

period, but spend the necessary time planning the Bible study sessions. Divide it into the 13 segments. Remember that the first few sessions are shorter than the last. For each participant, prepare a booklet in the form of a journal and include a reading assignment list. Be sure each participant owns a Bible. Have several Bible commentaries on hand at each session.

Each meeting should have the following ingredients: common ground time, report of past week, look at today's lesson, discussion, application and closing. Here is an outline for the initial meeting:

Session One

Begin *precisely* on time. This will alert late-comers that the group means business. If you want the young people to bring their Bibles, do not supply them at the study. They will get the message that they need to bring their own.

1. **Ring-up (5 minutes).** Ask God to come into your midst. Sit down in a circle.

2. **Common-ground time (10 minutes).** Allow time around the circle for each person to talk about who he or she really is and what his or her dreams are. You may do this by telling your story: Where you are from, how long you've lived in your area and your wildest dream. When everyone has had a chance to share, begin a circle-sentence sharing.

3. **Circle-sentence sharing (15 minutes).** You, the leader, should begin by talking about why you believe a Bible study is important and why you want to participate in this one. Invite the participants to complete the sentence, "I want to be in this Bible study because . . ." Go around the circle and let each person participate. Remind the youth that they must complete the sentence with a few words, not with a paragraph, essay or short story. Go around the circle three times. Each round with the same sentence completion will get deeper and

deeper.

4. Bible study introduction (5 minutes). You as the leader should give an introduction to the Bible study by explaining how it is going to take place each week. Be sure to talk about growth and the change that takes place in us when we study and apply the Bible in our lives. Change is growth. Review the guidelines of the contract stressing being on time, reading the lesson, avoiding put-downs, making application and being accountable.

5. Writing the credo (15 minutes). Have everyone write a credo (a statement of basic beliefs). Explain that we all believe something. Give some guidelines for writing a credo. They are as follows:

Write a paragraph about each one of the following
    areas of belief:
About God, I believe . . .
About Jesus, I believe . . .
About the Holy Spirit, I believe . . .
About the Bible, I believe . . .
About the church, I believe . . .
About humanity, I believe . . .
About family, I believe . . .
About sin, I believe . . .

6. Closing (10 minutes). The last 10 minutes should be spent explaining and giving background material on the specific Bible study. (For your Bible study, choose from your denominational material or resources that your pastor recommends.) Make assignments, then "ring-up" and offer a prayer of thanksgiving, praise and mercy.

Sessions two through 13 follow much the same pattern as the initial one with four exceptions:

● Review and report on how the scripture from the last study was applied in their lives. Do this at the beginning of each session following common-ground time; the leader should report on how he or she applied the scripture that was studied the past week. Give each participant a chance to do the same.

● At the conclusion of each study session, each teenager should write in his or her journal what he or she learned from the study. After most have finished, ask for volunteers to share with the group how they will apply what they've learned to their lives in the week to come.

For example, perhaps your Bible study is the parable of the talents (Matthew 25:14-30). After studying and discussing, ask each person to identify the talent that he or she has hidden and determine how he or she will uncover it in the coming week. Be specific.

● In the last session, ask each one of the members to write his or her new credo. This credo is a duplicate of the one they filled out at the initial session. When the new credos are turned in, appointments should be scheduled with the leader to discuss personal growth. This is a fun process. I like to have students read a part of the new credo, such as, "I believe about God . . ." Then I read the corresponding part from the old credo. The comparison between the old and new credos is often striking and usually encouraging to the students.

● The last session may be designated for celebration. If not, plan for still another session to celebrate the personal and community growth. Whether you have a party, banquet, or a get-together, be sure to include a worship time and give everyone a chance to answer the following open-ended responses:

From this study I learned . . .

My biggest surprise came when . . .

My future is going to be better by . . .

I believe God wants me to respond to his Word by . . .

Offering Bible studies in 13-week segments has many advantages. There is a beginning and an end; people can become a part of a Bible study at different times during the year; and a person can get some rest from group study and not feel guilty. Most exciting is the change in people that often happens in effective Bible study.

A RELATIONAL BIBLE STUDY METHOD

At one of Lyman Coleman's first Serendipity workshops several years ago, I learned a simple and effective Bible study method that works well with youth. Lyman gave each of us a paper cup and split us into groups of four. "Do with this cup what you would like to see happen to the church," he said. "We'll do this in silence and then give each person an opportunity to share why he shaped the cup the way he did."

Common objects such as paper cups help people to focus their abstract thoughts on a specific piece of reality. Learning takes place as people struggle creatively to express their thoughts and feelings. They usually go beyond thinking about the object. The paper cup, for example, is simply a way to help people express their feelings about the church. When they talk about their cup, they are *actually* talking about the church.

One benefit of attending events such as Serendipity workshops is the opportunity to "steal" ideas for use in your own church. I stole Lyman's idea (which he probably stole from someone else) and used it in one of my youth Sunday school classes at a Louisiana church.

The Rebels Class in my church had named themselves. They did their best to live up to their class name. They didn't want to study the life and teachings of Jesus or the journeys of Paul. They wanted to spend Sunday school in their cars listening to eight-track tape decks and chewing and smoking tobacco. But they also had a desire to sort out who they were and where they were going. The "leader of the pack" asked me to teach a class on "problems we have everyday." I thought it might be a good experiment to try the Rebels Class. We decided to meet in my office.

The Rebels Class struggled along for a few weeks. I
didn't think we had accomplished much of anything positive. Each week seemed a forum for expressing anger
and rebellion. The big change happened when I used
the paper cup idea from the Serendipity workshop. I explained that the cup was the church and to do with the
cup what they would like to see happen to the church. I
decided to alter the idea by using just one cup and
passing it around the circle.

I could see excitement in the group. They could
hardly wait to get hold of the cup. I gave the cup to the
first guy sitting next to me. He said, "Are you sure you
want us to do what you just said?"

"Yes, but you must do it in silence. Then we'll talk
about it," I said.

He then put the cup down on the floor, stood up, and
came down hard on it with his foot and crushed it. He
then handed the cup to the girl sitting next to him. She
tore the cup into tiny pieces. She handed all those
pieces to the girl sitting next to her, who tore each
piece in half. She passed the little giblets in her hand to
Bruce, who was sitting next to a door that opened to
the parking lot. Bruce opened the door, stepped out a
little, made a neat pile of paper pieces on the parking
lot, pulled his lighter out of his pocket and lit the cup on
fire. Everyone watched as the "church" burned. When
the smoke had cleared, everyone looked at me.

Bruce broke the silence and said, "Okay, now what?"

"Pass it, " I said.

He looked puzzled but knew I was serious. He
gathered up the ashes and handed them to the girl sitting next to him. She searched through those ashes and
found one small piece of unburned paper. She took that
one piece and tore it in half. Then she handed the ashes
to Harold.

Harold weighed about 250 pounds always wore a suit
to church and sported a Sunday school attendance pin

on his lapel that his mother made him wear. Harold didn't ever say much. He talked, walked and thought slowly. As he held the ashes in his hands, you could almost hear the huge tumblers in his head trying to think of something to do.

His hands were shaped like the good hands of All-state. He brought his hands up slowly to his face and just as I thought he was about to do something very religious, he spit into his hands! Almost in unison, the class members said in disgust, "Grrroooss, Harold!"

Guess who was sitting next to Harold? I was so glad it was not me. It was Dianna. Dianna was the unspoken leader of the Rebels. She put her hand out to Harold like a real trooper. Harold gave a crooked grin, wiped all of that saliva, ashes and giblets of paper into one hand and then slapped his hand across her hand and made sure every bit of it was transferred. Dianna held her hand out until Harold had completed his task and then very slowly brought it back in toward her. She looked down at the spital. She looked up into the eyes of each person sitting in the circle, then looked back down. We watched until she used her index finger to move the spital around in her hand until she had made the symbol of a cross. I didn't understand it and no one else did either. In fact, the silence was broken immediately with questions like: "Dianna, why did you do that?"

"I can't believe that Dianna."

"What did you do that for?"

With a cold expression on her face and eyes that looked like they were ready to explode with tears, Dianna looked around the room at each one of us and said: "When the cup started with David, and then began to go around the room, I saw how each one of us destroyed the church in different ways. When it came to me in this condition, I didn't know what to do, but I knew something had to be done. So, I made a cross." I could have hugged her! We sat there for another 90 minutes talking about what the church really was. We read 1 Corinthians 12:12-27. We discussed how we are all different parts of the body and how we all have a different part to play. That day the church was born in the life of the Rebels Class.

I still see some of those Rebels. They're grown into adults, many have children and are very active in the church. They still ask, "Do you remember when Harold . . .?" I see them provide the church with strong leadership as they seek to grow as Christians. I'm still amazed that one small paper cup has had such a tremendous impact on so many lives.

A sense of faithful accomplishment comes with almost all kinds of Bible study. Certainly, Bible study is important. But the rewards of studying God's Word are so much fuller than feeling good. The potential of God speaking to your group through scripture and the life-altering possibilities are more than heart-rending. They are opportunities for discovering the truth and allowing the truth to set you free. That freedom allows for your young people to grow in relationship with one another. Make the study of God's word an integral part of your youth group's life.

Worship

A spiritual growth program without worship is like an orchestra without music. Worship is the celebration of what God has done for us in our lives. It is a reminder that God loves us and we love God. It is the acknowledgment that our strength comes from God. Rejoicing together creates warm hearts and motivates us to serve others.

If we are all members of Christ's body—"a fellowship of believers" (Romans 12)—then youth are full equals in church. As youth sponsors, directors, counselors or youth, we need to claim that. To claim equality is to seek to be a *part* not *apart*. Our ministries must reflect the desire to be a part of the total congregation.

In many churches this concept is not recognized as a viable one. "Youth are supposed to stay in their place and remain the future of the church." As long as our youth groups continue to isolate themselves by sitting in the back pews or in the balcony at worship services, we reinforce this incorrect notion.

Youth need to be involved in worship services. They need to participate in the services by reading scripture, saying prayers, ushering or making announcements. These acts give youth *visibility* in the congregation. Adults see that youth really can make a contribution. Visibility also helps youth build confidence and feel a part of the worship experience. With a little guidance, the most liturgical or ritualistic worship can reflect a sensitivity to youth. For example, simply having a young person on the worship planning committee endorses the importance of young people in the church.

As you try to make this transition, offer an education program for the youth. Make arrangements for adult leaders in the church to meet with the youth group and talk about their areas of ministry. Ask the adult leaders to give the youth an opportunity to make suggestions. Build a design for the educational program which encompasses the entire workings of the church—from the crib to the grave. Teach youth the function of the church and ask for their input and service. When you belong to something (have part in it) you not only support it, you want to be in the middle of the action.

The story below illustrates the truth that what we are involved in, we tend to support.

A certain woman in a southern state was leading the resistance to the beginning of the federal Headstart Program. She had rallied many people in the state to her persuasion. The government workers and politicians did not know how to handle her. The fate of the Headstart program was in question until one of the politicians came up with the plan to appoint her as the director of Headstart for the state. They offered her the job. She accepted it. The resistance suddenly disappeared. They got her involved in their program and she became an advocate instead of an enemy.

As absurd as is this true story, it points out how involvement often cures resistance. If youth are involved, worship will take on significant meaning to them.

Worship is important for the total congregation. Worship is also an important element of any youth group program. Age group (junior high and senior high) worship also is necessary. The following are three models of worship I've found successful for each of those settings.

TOTAL CONGREGATIONAL WORSHIP (DEEPER ROOTS)

I once worked for a church in which it was unusual to have more than 100 people in the Sunday evening worship service. One Sunday, however, there were more than 200. Had the publicity worked? Had the nature of the worship service attracted the extra 100 people? These people were expecting to discover some "Deeper Roots," the theme of a six-week series. All of our publicity—church newsletter, posters, committees, phone calls and personal contacts—promised "Deeper Roots."

Several weeks prior to the first "Deeper Roots" worship service, the senior pastor and I met to discuss youth involvement in the church. Meeting *first* with the senior pastor is crucial to the success of any youth-led worship service involving the entire congregation. Without patronizing him, I shared with my senior pastor the perceived real needs of the youth in our church. We reflected how those needs were similar among all of our people. We narrowed the top need for both young and older as a desire for a deeper faith. We then agreed to establish a task force of both youth and adults to plan worship services that addressed the perceived need for deeper faith. This task force was jointly appointed and given parameters for the worship services.

If you are inexperienced at organized youth-led worship services, I would strongly suggest starting out do-

ing only one service. As your task force is successful,
you may wish to attempt more ambitious undertakings.
Remember that it is best for all concerned to experience a modest success instead of a grandiose failure.

Once assembled, our task force set deadlines and assigned each person responsibilities such as publicity,
program, finances, etc. The time soon came for us to
carry out the first worship service of Deeper Roots.
As people filled the sanctuary, there was a growing air
of expectancy. They were ushered to their seats by the
light of a few candles. The only prominent light was
from a rear-screen projection showing a slide of a beautiful, colorful drawing: a cross-section of a tree putting
its roots down into the rich soil, searching for a cool
drink of water. The theme for the next six weeks was
written in bold print across the face of the slide. It simply said "Deeper Roots." The background music was a
combination of old church hymns and newer contemporary worship songs. Each tune was familiar to almost
everyone.

The slide on the rear-screen projection changed to
the words of our theme song: "That Cause Can Neither
Be Lost nor Stayed." Instead of using the hymnal, we
used sing-along slides that the youth group had made.
The organist accompanied and the congregation was
led by the song leader using an offstage microphone:

> *That cause can neither be lost nor stayed*
> *which takes the course of what God hath made*
> *and is not trusting in walls and towers,*
> *but slowly, growing from seeds to flowers.*

The mood was set. After singing the final verse, a
spotlight encircled me. I welcomed the congregation to
this service and explained that the next six weeks of
Sunday evening worship experiences were designed to
call our congregation to a deeper commitment of

prayer, Bible study, personal growth and service. I told
them that at the conclusion of the evening worship, they
would be challenged to make a pledge for six weeks of
deepening their spiritual roots.

The spotlight switched from me to our soloist as he
sang "Fill My Cup, Lord." Another spotlight focused in
the center of the room where a youth group member
began leading us in an evening prayer.

Following the prayer, the platform in the front of the
sanctuary lighted up. The youth group pantomimed the
parable of the good Samaritan as our pastor read the
scripture. At the conclusion of the scripture lesson, the
sanctuary again turned to darkness and the rear-screen
projection changed to sing-along slides of Anne
Murray's song "You Needed Me."

The spotlight was then shined on the pastor. He gave
a brief 15-minute meditation about the theme "Deeper
Roots" and how we need each other. He also told how
Christ can use us to be there for one another. I still remember his words so clearly as he concluded the
meditation:

"We invite all of you to a prayer time. Come down to
the altar as you wish, stay as long as you need, silently
dismiss yourselves, and return to your pew to meditate
or pray until the benediction. If you come tonight with a
special need or concern and would like one of us to
kneel and talk or pray with you here at the altar, simply lift your hand and one of us will be with you." (Arrangements had been made ahead of time for two senior high youth and one other adult to assist our pastor
behind the prayer rail. Each had been instructed what
to do.)

The pastor continued, "If any of you would like to
commit to the Deeper Roots program or learn more
about it, then please indicate so and we will meet in the
church library following this worship service. Here is
what it means to take the "Deeper Roots" challenge:

Pray daily, study the Bible daily, tithe, become part of a weekly share group, attend church and Sunday school regularly, witness to someone each day, do one unselfish act each day and keep a journal.

"Following the singing of our theme song, I invite you to come to the altar." I was moved as I watched the people pour from the pews and patiently wait in line for a spot at the altar.

After the service, the library was packed! I described the commitment for Deeper Roots and could hardly believe my eyes when many of the hands went up to receive pledge cards. Following is an example of our pledge card:

Deeper Roots

I _____ hereby pledge a deeper commitment to God by following these steps for the next six weeks of my life.

_____
from (date) to (date)

_____ 1. I will set aside a specific time each day to pray and follow the guidelines of Deeper Roots.

_____ 2. I will read and study the scripture daily following the suggestions in Deeper Roots.

_____ 3. I will tithe 10 percent of my time, talents, treasure and tongue for six weeks.

_____ 4. I will participate in a weekly share group for the next six weeks.

_____ 5. I will attend worship and church school class every Sunday during this six-week period.

_____ 6. I will tell someone about my experience with Christ each day.

_____ 7. I will do one unselfish act each day.

____ 8. I will keep my Deeper Roots journal up-to-date each day.

Signed _____

Address_____ Phone_____

They could take a deeper walk in faith by selecting one or more of the eight steps listed on the pledge card. I was not surprised to discover that almost everyone chose to do *all* eight steps. As we collected the pledge cards, the Deeper Roots journals were passed out. We handed out more than 75 that first night. We had only printed 100; now we anticipated that many more would be needed.

We explained that the journals included a facsimilie of the pledge card, a thorough explanation of each of the eight steps, and a journal page for each day of the six-week period. Following is an example of a journal page:

Date _____

Today I prayed _____

_____

_____

Read _____.* In your own words what does this scripture hold for you? What action are you going to take as a result of this scripture? _____

_____

_____

My unselfish act today was _____

_____

_____

I witnessed today to one other person by_____
_____
_____

**My share group is helping me grow by _____
_____
_____

    *Choose a scripture passage for each day of the 30 days. **One day per week, this entry should be included in the journal.

    Next, we made assignments to share groups according to neighborhoods. In all cases, the new Deeper Roots converts rallied to take turns leading the sharing and offering their homes for the meetings.

    This was a wonderful night in the life of our church. The nights that followed were equally as wonderful. Regular worship services followed the exact format for the entire six-week period. At each service, various people gave testimonies on how their Deeper Roots commitment was affecting their lives. We had over 250 people step forward to take the Deeper Roots pledge. Each worship service grew in size and by the last night, more than 600 people filled the sanctuary! Our annual church budget was met by the additional giving of those 250 people who signed the pledge. The unselfish acts, the spirit of the people, and the growth of relationships were talked about for months after Deeper Roots.

    I was excited by seeing the program planned and carried out in large part by our youth department. The involvement of youth and adults in the planning, implementation and commitment to Deeper Roots created a new understanding, awareness and appreciation of the possibilities of youth in total church involvement.

YOUTH GROUP WORSHIP (REACH OUT)

Worship is an important element in any successful
youth group. While it is true that congregational worship is the most important, youth groups also need to
worship. In my years of professional youth ministry, one
very successful model of youth group worship has
worked in every congregation I've served. I call it a
Reach Out service.

The Reach Out service is a monthly experience that
integrates witness, prayer, and commitment in a powerful and community-building setting. The purpose is to
praise God and affirm each other. The goal, of course, is
spiritual growth. As with any youth group worship activity, several key points need to be kept in mind as the
Reach Out service is planned and carried out. First, it
must be held regularly in order to gain a sense of ritual. Second, it should have a fairly consistent format.
Third, it must be planned and done *with* youth, not *for*
them. The youth worker needs to deflate his or her ego
and release control and ownership to the young people.

The setting for the Reach Out service should be a
chapel or sanctuary. Here is an example of an agenda:

- Meet with helpers (In the chapel, form a commitment circle and pray. At first, I am usually the only one
who prays; but after a while, I invite anyone who
wishes to pray to do so. This commitment circle is precious and sets the stage for the real ministry to take
place. We ask God to be with us during the Reach Out
service. We hug each other in the circle and very
quietly slip away to our responsibilities.)
- Begin background music, lower the lights, light the
candles
  - Usher the youth group members to their seats
  - Prayer
  - Special music
  - Facilitator presentation:
  1. Orientation of the Reach Out service

2. Share a personal experience with God
3. Invite others to share
4. Invite congregation to prayer time
● Altar prayer time
● Self-dismissal to fellowship hall for refreshments (The refreshment time is a chance for emotional release and fellowship and is an important ingredient to the overall concept of the Reach Out service.)

Picture the last hour of your youth meeting. Announcements have been made throughout the last few weeks about the upcoming Reach Out service and now the time for it has come. Ask the youth group members to begin singing a familiar song such as "Pass It One," "Kumbaya," or "We Are the Reason" then quietly lead the students toward the chapel.

A team of youth help every month with the Reach Out service. Following are descriptions of the helper's responsibilities and further explanation of the Reach Out service:

1. **Inside usher.** (There are usually one or two depending on size of group.) Signal the beginning to the outside usher. Stand at the front of the chapel and seat worshipers close together (beginning at the front pew). As soon as one pew is filled, step toward the next pew and fill it too. When all have sat down, sit on the last pew on which people are seated.

2. **Outside usher.** Do not allow anyone into the chapel until everyone is quiet. Wait for the signal from the inside usher. When everyone is quiet, give instructions to go in (very quietly) to the front and follow the directions of the inside usher. When everyone is inside, follow and sit on the last pew on which people are seated.

3. **Youth who has prayer.** Plan the prayer prior to worship service. Meet with the youth director or person in charge to go over the prayer and get suggestions. Following the commitment circle, slip out of the chapel and join the rest of the group. Place yourself toward the

middle of the group so that you will be near the center of the whole group. When everyone is seated and the music has ceased, stand where you are and begin praying. Do not say "let us pray," just begin.

4. Special music person. The youth director or coordinator will help you choose a song. Following the prayer, the music begins. A song may be sung or it may be instrumental. In either case, position yourself in an inconspicuous place such as the balcony, or behind the altar. This ensures that the focus is not diverted from the worship setting.

5. Facilitator. (This responsibility is usually the youth director's for the first few times. It can and should be handed over to others as their leadership emerges.) When the music is over, stand in the center of the platform in plain sight of everyone. It is important that you be as close as possible to the total group. Begin by explaining the purpose of the Reach Out service. Say: "In a moment each one of us will have an opportunity to share our victories in Christ as well as express any doubts that we might have concerning the faith. No one will be put down. That's a rule. The hope is that as we share, our hearts will be open to one another and reach out in love and action. I don't know what is going to happen, but this is a moment for us to trust God and reach out to one another."

After communicating the purpose of the Reach Out service, model what you are asking everyone else to do by going first. Have in mind an experience in which you recently have had a specific encounter with God (or in which God spoke to you). The more vulnerable you are in front of your youth group, the more they will feel free to share. Consequently, the depth of the Reach Out service usually depends on the vulnerability of the facilitator.

When you finish sharing, invite others to discuss their victories or doubts. You may do so by saying some-

thing such as, "Now, it's your turn." Remind the youth
that all answers are acceptable and no one will be put
down. Tell them to stand when they are ready to share.
Note that it is a scary thing for a person to stand in
front of a group and share. It sometimes takes a while
to get up the courage to stand as well as gather
thoughts about what to say. Do not be impatient—just
remain in front of the group and wait. The first few
times you attempt this service you may want to ask several people (prior to the service) to be ready to share so
they can "get the ball rolling." This helps others feel
comfortable in their sharing.

After each one shares, offer a word of appreciation
or affirmation such as: "I know that was hard to share.
Thank you." "Thank you. We all have been there."
"That's neat." "I really appreciate that." "God bless
you."

Before long, with your continued affirmation and
spiritual focus, the group will look forward to this worship more than anything else during the month. The
sharing will become almost impossible to stop!

The facilitator is the time keeper. *Do not* let this service go on forever. Sometimes the tendency is to let the
sharing go on as long as it is going well. People tire,
Moms and Dads have to wait and the momentum will
disappear. Plan a time for the Reach Out service and
stick to it. It is always better to quit while you're ahead
than to push your luck! I suggest 30 minutes for the
first share time with the last 10 minutes set aside for
personal prayers. When closing the sharing, state that,
"We have time for just a couple of more to share . . ."
This statement serves as a motivator for those who
have not yet had the courage to share to go ahead. This
statement also makes the point that the share time is
almost over.

When the last person has shared, give an invitation
for everyone to come to the altar and pray. Instruct

them to come, stay as long as they like, then dismiss themselves and meet in the youth room for refreshments and informal fellowship.

Tell the students that if anyone would like to rededicate his or her life to Christ, make a profession of faith or talk about a problem to "Come, kneel, and silently lift your hand and one of the people behind the prayer rail will kneel and pray or talk very quietly with you. The altar is now open for prayer."

Go down to the prayer rail and pray first, then return to your place behind the prayer rail. Space yourself and other prayer helpers in order to service and minister to anyone in front of them who lifts his or her hand. When everyone has prayed, and the chapel is empty, go to the youth room for refreshments.

6. Prayer helpers. (There are usually two or three helpers.) When the facilitator calls the group to prayer time, kneel and pray first. Then take your place behind the prayer rail. As participants lift their hands, simply kneel quietly in front of them, ask how you can help, then prayerfully follow your instincts. This is a little scary at first but it is so rewarding to be God's vehicle.

7. Background music. Preferably, music should be playing quietly as everyone comes into the chapel. When everyone is seated, the music stops. Begin again during prayer time and continue to play until everyone has gone. Be sure to choose devotional-type music. Your selection of music and the manner in which you play is one of the most important elements in the Reach Out service.

8. Worship setting people. Often, the worship setting is live. This "live setting" is used from the time people come in until the special music is complete. As the facilitator stands to pray, quickly have a seat on the front row. Be sure the inside usher saves a spot for you.

The worship setting is a "live sculpture." Using a scripture passage, think of some ways to use two or three people to sculpture that passage. A scripture sculpture features three or four people who think of creative ways to "freeze" themselves in a sculpture-like pose of a passage. Most all of the parables of Jesus lend themselves to this form: the Good Samaritan (Luke 10:25-37), The Prodigal Son (Luke 15:11-32), The Lost Coin (Luke 15:8-10) and many others.

Have the live sculpture get into position just before the doors are open for admission into the chapel. A spotlight with colored jells lends some extra inspiration and excitement.

Try the Reach Out service with your group. This monthly worship service will help to unify your group and provide a regular avenue for spiritual nourishment.

AGE GROUP WORSHIP

Regular worship experiences for age groups can and usually do become challenging and powerful. Age group worship, unlike regular church worship, focuses on the specific individual needs within a youth group—"touching the members where they hurt." Careful planning for one of these experiences is crucial. Everything must be taken into consideration to "hit the mark."

This worship concentrates on the needs of young people. How does one discover their needs? One way I learn is to sit around with young people and talk about their wants and hopes. Then I ask them how God can make a difference. I ask, "How could we demonstrate to the youth group in worship that God has an answer?" I'm always pleasantly surprised and inspired by their answers and ideas.

A Model for Senior High (Rita)

Several years ago, as I was employing this process, our group came up with one of the most dynamic worship experiences I have ever done or seen. We simply called it "Rita."

In a previous conversation, someone observed that he knew many people who were only interested in making money, having sex and being popular. Someone else said, "That's a dead-end street. What we have in youth group is much more important than that!" We talked about how material things did not meet up to our expectations. There was something missing. We knew it was God. How could we graphically show that? How could we challenge people to move in that direction? Our answer was Rita.

Following is a basic outline of Rita's story. For your "Rita" service, elaborate according to your youth group members' needs: Rita is a typical, popular teenager with both bad and good things happening to her. She had a great senior year in high school; however, when she gets to college, things begin to fall apart. She has no close friends, she loses her boyfriend, she is away from her family and classes are too much. Alone in her room, she contemplates suicide and finally can stand it no more. There is nothing. No one to call on. She takes her life.

As a youth group community, we need each other. We need God. As we are friends for each other, God is there. God is in us, showing himself to the world.

For this powerful service, you will need the following materials:

1. **Rita.** A life-size, unfired piece of ceramic greenware resembling a human head. A local ceramic store probably has exactly what you need. There is a "Samoan girl" that is usually always in stock that will do very well. Be careful with her, she is fragile.

2. **Tempera paint.** You will need red, yellow, orange, blue, green and black. Mix each color in a separate four-ounce paper cup. Make sure the mixture is thick so that it can be poured slowly out of the cup.

3. **Recorded music.** Select contemporary music that you believe meets the needs of the various parts of the

worship service.

4. Spotlight. This is optional. You can make your own spotlight from a headlight or use a sealed beam lantern.

5. French bread. This will be used at the conclusion of the worship.

6. Other needs. Hammer, small table, two trays, two white cloths: one to cover Rita and one to cover the bread, off-stage public address system (optional), straw and "The Hollow Men" by T.S. Eliot.

The Rita service begins with music quietly playing as the youth group enters the room. The only light is from a spotlight focused on a small table with "Rita" sitting on a tray covered by a white cloth.

The narrator stands behind Rita, takes off the cloth and tells her story. Begin Rita's story at the lowest grade level of your members; for example, "When Rita entered her freshman year in high school, she was the happiest girl in the world. Things were going so well for her."

While you are talking about Rita's happiness, one of your helpers comes across the stage, pauses next to Rita and very slowly pours some of the yellow tempera paint over her head. The color yellow represents the happiness of joy. As the paint runs down over Rita's face continue telling her story. Make up your own story about Rita based on the characteristics of your group. Tell about events that did not work out: failed tests, broken relationships with friends, fights with Mom and Dad. Also tell about events that went well: school prom, election to cheerleader and so forth.

As you mention each event in Rita's life, have someone come up to Rita and pour a color over her head. Let the colors represent the feelings: blue and black—sorrow and pain; red—anger; yellow, orange and green—various degrees of joy and contentment. By the time Rita is "in college," everyone in the room will identify with her in some way. As you begin to talk about Rita in college, use more dismal stories—everything was going wrong. She lost her boyfriend, got poor grades, her roommate was stealing from her, etc.

Conclude the story: "Rita sat on the side of her bed. There was no one. She had never been so depressed in her life. She seemed to be hemmed in from all sides. Rita picked up the bottle of sleeping pills next to her bed and . . ." At this point, slip your hand behind the table and pick up the hidden hammer. Hit the clay head. The greenware will shatter into many pieces. The effect of this action is powerful! So many have identified with Rita that it is like the end for them.

After the hammer comes down, the spotlight goes off. (Turn on a strobe light and play loud rock music that almost pierces the ears. If you do not have a strobe, experiment with someone rapidly turning the lights on and off.) Rita will be demolished and, if you have filled the sculpture with straw, people could shout out such things as: "She's empty!" "There's nothing there!" "She's filled with straw!"

As the music subsides, read T.S. Eliot's "The Hollow Men." Allow one minute for the music to fade. When the music has completely died and everyone is in total darkness, play a song that lifts up God as our purpose to live such as "We Are the Reason" by David Meece. Bring up the music gradually until it fills the entire room. The spotlight comes up simultaneously with the music.

Instead of the broken Rita, another object is on the table covered with a white cloth. (The trays are switched during the darkness.) As "We Are the Reason" fades, begin talking about the new life we have in Christ. Talk about how Christ is someone we can count on. Talk about being friends for one another and sharing life with each other. As you talk, uncover the loaf of bread on the table. Talk about the bread of life as you break it and give it to someone. Demonstrate

feeding another as you talk about God feeding us
through each other. While the bread is being passed
form person to person, lead the group in songs such as:
"Pass It On," "Amazing Grace," "Take Our Bread" or
"Father, We Adore You."

Conclude the worship with a ring-up. Ask everyone to
put their arms around each other in a circle. Lead the
group in prayer, and a rededication such as, "All that I
am and all that I have, I give to Christ and to his
service."

A Model for Junior High (Take Up the Cross)

The Rita worship service is by nature more effective
with senior high students. Senior high students are
more able to grasp symbolic and abstract concepts.
Junior high students tend to think in more concrete and
specific terms. In the case of Rita, senior high kids
would understand that the colors poured on her head
were symbolic of her emotions. Junior high kids would
be amused that a piece of ceramic was getting gooey
paint poured on it.

For junior high students, highly specific worship is
more effective. For example, I've always had good experiences with "Take Up the Cross," a very specific worship service that's based on Mark 8:34, "If anyone
would come after me, he must deny himself and take up
up his cross and follow me." I interpret denying yourself as acting in the interest of what's best for other
people. When we truly deny ourselves we are free to be
happy as we "do unto others."

For this worship, you will need small candles, about
the size of a finger (one for each participant). Make a
cross of lumber or tree limbs. Using a drill about the
same size as your candles, drill holes at 45 degree
angles on the vertical and horizontal parts of the cross.
You also will need a metal trash can, index cards, pens,
cardboard, heat-absorbing mat, background music,

matches and one large candle. Set the cross up on an angle to avoid burning the candles too quickly.

This service works best as a concluding experience for meetings or retreats dealing with commitment to Christ. It's also good for using with New Year's Eve gatherings on resolutions for the coming year.

Begin the service with special music already playing as the junior high students enter the place of worship. Everyone is to be quiet—no talking. As the music ends, *briefly* summarize the retreat's or meeting's teaching. I usually say something like: "We've talked about denial as putting others ahead of ourselves for God's sake. We've talked about how Jesus did this and what it means to be a Christian. It's time for us to go home. What is the next step you need to take? What do you need to do in your life so that others are put first? What is one thing you are doing in your life that you need to be rid of?"

Pass out index cards and pens. With music playing quietly, have the participants silently write the thing they're going to give over to God in order to better follow Christ. When everyone is finished, invite them to come forward to the cross, one at a time. Each person is to take an unlighted candle from the cross and light it with the large candle. At this point he or she may choose to share what is written on the card. Make it clear that sharing what he or she wrote on the card is totally voluntary. To show that it's okay not to share, you should go first and not share what you wrote. Set the card on fire and drop it into the trash can.

The next adult who comes forward should say what's on the card so that the young people understand how to say what's necessary. He or she then sets fire to the card with the small candle and carefully drops it into the metal trash can. Make sure to cover the carpet to avoid wax drippings. Cardboard works well for this purpose. Also be sure to place a heat-absorbing mat under the trash can to avoid damaging the floor. After the adult places his or her burning card in the trash can, he or she places the small candle back into the cross. Allow time for every junior high student to come up to the cross, light his or her candle, burn the card and place the candle back into the cross. Turn out all the lights. The cross usually lights up the room well. Close the worship with an eye-open prayer.

8

Prayer and Meditation

Dr. Peele called me into his office. A youth director whose senior minister insists on being called "Dr." or "Reverend" all of the time has an interpersonal relationship problem. I had been the youth director for only six months and had continually gotten flak from the "front office." Usually it was about attendance or a function of my job that had not been fully discussed with me. This time was different. He wanted *me* in his office. That spelled S-C-A-R-E-D.

"Please sit down," he said. "I'll get right to the point. Several youth have been cutting out of Sunday school and coming over to the education building prior to worship every Sunday for the past several weeks. They've been rummaging around over there in some of the vacant classrooms. I suspect they are smoking or at least hiding out. I want it stopped. We have to have better control than that! Do you understand me?"

I choked and said, "Yes sir, but . . ."

"No buts about it!" the senior pastor exclaimed.

"Dr. Peele, those kids are not slipping out of Sunday school," I explained. "I have been dismissing them 15 minutes early so they can get to the old Baxter classroom for prayer before the 11 a.m. worship service. Eleven of our kids have been meeting there to pray for you and the worship service."

I knew Dr. Peele had his doubts about what I had just told him, but I also knew he had exaggerated his charges against the youth. I had met with them several times in the beginning. Dr. Peele rolled his eyes and said, "I don't think those are the same kids . . . check on it; and if it's not stopped, stop it."

"Yes sir," I said.

A couple of Sundays passed without incident. Then one Sunday morning as Dr. Peele was on his way to the sanctuary to lead worship, he passed the old Baxter classroom. The door was ajar. He heard youthful voices and immediately became suspicious. But then he saw the youth sitting in a circle, holding hands and praying for him and the church. He quietly slipped in and broke the chain of hands. Our senior pastor joined in the prayer time. After a few moments, he slipped out.

In the worship service that followed, Dr. Peele appeared to be a new man. His opening remarks were: "Do you people have any idea that while you have been sitting here the last few minutes that about a dozen of our *fine* young people have been praying for you, for me and this worship service? We would all do well to learn from this wonderful group of youth. We have the finest youth in America and I'm proud to be their pastor."

As pompous as some of this may have sounded, it ignited a new appreciation of youth in the life of our church. We took advantage of it. At every turn we had youth doing something positive for the congregation.

The war was not over in getting recognition for youth in the total involvement of the church, but a major battle had been won.

The above example is only one of many prayer projects you can do that can turn your church around and create a new, positive attitude about youth and their abilities. Let me tell you how we turned a very negative attitude on the part of the youth into a positive, powerful influence.

In a "rap 'n snac" (refreshment time after a youth group meeting), it became apparent that a negative attitude toward the church and the pastor was surfacing. Some of the youth complained that the pastor and other church staff were always making snide comments about them: the way they dressed, how they were disruptive in the church office area, etc. I had to admit that most of the charges were true. But, they were just being youth. The youth group members dressed comfortably after school and they had a lot of energy. It was unfortunate that my office was in the middle of the rest of the staff offices. I was unsure about what I could do to improve the situation. I wanted the youth to feel free to visit with me in my office, but I did not want to be continually putting down the wrath of the church staff. As the conversation continued, someone finally asked, "Well, what can we do?" One of our college-age counselors suggested "behavior modification."

After explaining behavior modification as a way of changing our own behavior and also working to change others' behavior, we decided to empower our newly found concept with the use of prayer.

It was decided that we would begin a daily prayer ritual. Each day after school, beginning at 3:15 p.m. and continuing until 5 p.m., someone would be at the chapel altar praying specifically for the church staff and their relationship with the youth. At the same time, we each would be as sensitive as we could in our behavior in the office area. We agreed to speak cheerfully with staff members, look for ways to affirm them, hold our noise down the best we could and offer to help in their ministries.

The behavior-modification prayer plan worked miracles! From the first day we saw results. Several days later, when I walked into the church office, I was overwhelmed. There was no way to think there had ever been a problem. Four young people were huddled with the membership secretary, working together to get a mailing out to the congregation. Everyone was laughing and having a good time. The pastor even came through the office area and instead of complaining about how the youth were dressed, he remarked that one of the guys really looked comfortable in the sweat shirt and he wished he could wear one to work. Later, those youth gave him a sweat shirt with his name on it. Prayer works when you put feet to it.

Debriefing prayer projects is an important function because we learn more about how to pray and we feel the power of prayer as we share results. After a debriefing period, those kids who changed the staff attitude began to look around for other prayer projects. There have been many since then. Prayer projects are contagious.

GUIDED FANTASY MEDITATION

A guided fantasy meditation is an effective means to help young people improve their self-image. This happens when they imagine themselves in a greater positive relationship with God. The common elements:

1. Close your eyes and imagine yourself in a solitary setting of beauty such as a deserted beach.

2. Jesus aproaches you in your setting.

3. Your encounter with Jesus is warm and positive.

4. When ready, you return to the present and evaluate the meaning of the guided fantasy.

Barbara Campbell, Orange, California, contributed
the following guided fantasy meditation. Appropriate
settings for this meditation are in quiet times at retreats and after the conclusions of a program. The
mood should be reflective. Ask the the youth to assume
a relaxed position and close their eyes. Then ask them
to inhale a deep breath and exhale slowly. Repeat
twice. Guide the group with the following meditation:

"I'd like to invite you to call to mind someone for
whom you would like to pray—someone you feel concern for and wish to bring to God in a special way. This
would best be someone close enough to you that you
can readily see in your imagination . . . perhaps someone in your family, school or youth group . . . It may be
a close personal friend who is significant in your life
and growth.

"In your imagination, begin to picture that special
person alone on a beautiful beach. It's cool, but not
cold. The sun is warm and the ocean breeze fills your
senses.

"Call to mind any unique habits and traits that you
always notice in your special person when you're
together . . . perhaps a favorite phrase or expression, a
special smile or touch.

"Call to mind the personal qualities you most appreciate in your special person . . . that quality might be
compassion, gentleness, thoughtfulness, honesty or enthusiasm . . . Focus on two or three of those qualities
that are most special to you in the way your person
touches your life.

"Now in your imagination, picture a stranger walking
slowly to your friend . . . As the stranger draws nearer,
you recognize him as Jesus . . . Imagine Jesus sitting
down with your friend—just as you might do if you
were going to be with him or her right now . . . See
Jesus placing his arm around your special person, or
reaching out his hands and making a special sign of

how glad he is to be with your friend today . . . Picture
the pleased look on your special person's face as he or
she looks into Jesus' eyes and soaks in the warmth and
strength that is so much a part of who Jesus is for each
of us.

"Take a moment to thank the Lord as he sits with
your special person, and for being there . . . Then thank
him for all the unique traits and qualities that you
notice in your special person.

"Now begin to visualize the Lord embracing your special person with all the warmth and compassion that
you could ever imagine.

"Then imagine Jesus departing and slowly disappear-
ing down the beach.

"And now imagine an empty space next to you . . .
Someone sits next to you, filling the empty space . . . Sitting next to you is the same Jesus who was just with
your special person. He's come to thank you for bring-
ing your special person to him in this way . . . He's taking your hands and looking into your eyes as he tells
you of his gratitude for this space and time that you've
given him . . . You lean back to relax together as he
puts his arm around your shoulders and goes on to tell
you of his appreciation for your openness to his loving
presence.

"You respond by telling Jesus your love for him . . .
You thank Jesus for his presence in your life and in the
life of your special person . . .

"When you are ready to bring your time together
with Jesus to a close and return to our group, open your
eyes."

At the close of this exercise, have the members list
on a 3×5 card or perhaps in their journal, the name of
their special person. Also, list the three or four qualities they most appreciated about him or her. Invite
them to write a letter of appreciation during the next
week to their special person.

JESUS IS ...

In another activity, have the group list on a chalk-
board or newsprint some of the qualities that they most
appreciate about a trusted friend. Ask that the qualities
be phrased in "the first person" such as: "She listens
to me," "He is there when I need him," "She loves me
even when I'm unlovable" and so on. Be sure to list
these qualities as they're expressed and offer no
comments.

After everyone has had a chance to make a contribution and the list is complete, say, "Let's take a look inside ourselves and think about the characteristics of
the Jesus whom we know. As we look at the qualities
we appreciated most in our friends, put the name of
Jesus in front of each one. For example, "Jesus listens
to me," "Jesus is there when I need him," "Jesus loves
me even when I am unlovable." Do this until you have
gone through the complete list.

This activity shows us that the same qualities that we
appreciate in our friends are the same qualities and
characteristics of Christ. It is the life we "live" that
shows what Christianity is and that *we* can be the
Christ to each other in our daily lives.

Retreats

The longing of young people to gain spiritual nourishment is too often not met in the traditional settings of Sunday school classes and religious education classes. If a young person were to attend all 52 Sunday school classes in a year, at an average of an hour each, he or she would have received 52 hours of guidance.

Statistically, however, young people attend only about half the Sunday services in a year—or about 26 hours.

With such a limited time in the structured service, I suggest that we use Sundays for systematic study and use retreats to emphasize spirituality and community building,

Phil Baker, Walt Marcum and Janie Lyman, led a team of 100 young people and designed a weekend retreat.

The design team specifically included the following in the retreat:
- Family building
- Journaling

- Praying
- Bible study (experiential)
- Fasting
- Meditation (experiential)
- Worship
- Spiritual growth gathering

The design team developed a student booklet and leader's guide. The following material is the leader's guide for the retreat. Each student's booklet should include several blank sheets of paper and copies of the following pages of the leader's guide: "My Spiritual Autobiography" and all four prayer journal assignments.

Retreat Schedule

Friday

7:00 p.m.	Registration
8:00 p.m.	Orientation
8:10 p.m.	Crowdbreakers
8:45 p.m.	Community Experience
9:00 p.m.	Spiritual Family Session
10:45 p.m.	Break
11:30 p.m.	Worship
12:45 a.m.	In rooms
1:15 a.m.	Bed check and lights out

Saturday

8:00 a.m.	Breakfast
8:45 a.m.	Worship
9:15 a.m.	Solitude
10:00 a.m.	Community Experience
10:30 a.m.	Spiritual Family Session
12:30 p.m.	Lunch
1:15 p.m.	Recreation
3:00 p.m.	Worship
3:30 p.m.	Solitude

5:00 p.m.	Free time
6:00 p.m.	Supper
6:30 p.m.	Community Experience
7:00 p.m.	Spiritual Family Session
9:00 p.m.	Dance
11:45 p.m.	End dance
Midnight	In rooms
1:00 a.m.	Bed check and lights out

Sunday

8:00 a.m.	Breakfast
9:00 a.m.	Solitude
9:30 a.m.	Community Experience
10:00 a.m.	Spiritual Family Session
11:15 a.m.	Solitude
11:30 a.m.	Closing worship

Following is a detailed description of the retreat schedule:

FRIDAY EVENING
Is *Something Missing?*

Registration (1 hour). Assign rooms, distribute pencils and student booklets. Organize activities such as volleyball, frisbee, hikes, etc.

Orientation (10 minutes). Welcome all of the students to the retreat. Briefly review the rules, schedule and student booklets.

Crowdbreakers (35 minutes). Offer a time for the group members to get to know each other. Sing songs such as "A-La, La, La, La, La, La, La, Le, Lu, Jah" and "Hallelu, Hallelu."[1] Play games such as "Symbolic Gifts," "Long Yarn," "If I Could" or "Designer Jeans."[2]

---

[1] **Songs** (San Anselmo, CA: Songs and Creation, 1978), pp. 12, 88.
[2] **Try This One**, Vol. I-IV (Loveland, CO: Group Books).

An example of a crowdbreaker is: Divide into small groups of six to eight students. Ask the small groups to form circles. Have each person share:

1. His or her name.
2. One bit of personal information that no one else knows.
3. Something he or she has found that has helped him or her feel closer to God in the past.
4. A word or image that describes each person's relationship with God right now.
5. Why he or she came this weekend and what he or she hopes to receive.

Go around the circle once for each of the questions. This will give the group members time to think about their answers and keep the sharing moving without focusing too much or too little on anyone.

In this manner, you begin at a comfortable, non-threatening pace and then move the group members toward sharing and talking openly about their relationships with God. This kind of sharing may be new and difficult for some of your group members.

You're trying to set the tone for your group for the rest of the sessions, so keep the group moving toward sharing without pushing too hard.

Community Experience

Guided Fantasy (15 minutes). Ask for some of the youth to read aloud John 1:1-5, 8:14, 16-18.

Explain that you will be taking the youth on a guided fantasy based on these verses. Ask the youth to relax, close their eyes, listen and imagine as you guide them. Slowly say the following:

"God is the creator and source of all that is. God is your creator. God gave the gift of life to you. Experience the preciousness and sacredness of that gift . . .

"God has been present all of your life. In some ways, you have known that and responded. Think of a time

when you felt close to God . . . Feel God's joy and love
at that moment . . . In many ways, we have missed that
presence. We've not known God—not accepted God.
Think of a time when you felt cut off from God—distant
and alone. Feel God's sadness at that moment . . .

"God is here with you now—in the world, in your life.
You can come to know God. Experience God's presence
in a way you never dreamed possible . . . God offers
grace to you—power to become what God wishes. Fantasize what your relationship with God could be . . .
What is God's wish for you? How do you feel?"

Spiritual Family Session
Spiritual Autobiography (15 minutes). To move
toward a deeper level of sharing, have the group members take 10 to 15 minutes to write a spiritual autobiography—a history of their relationship with God.

Ask the students to open their booklets to "My Spiritual Autobiography" (see below). Explain that they are
to focus on their faith journey—their relationship with
God as best as they are aware of it—and what has
helped or hindered that relationship. The autobiographies don't have to be in complete sentences. The students are to strive for insights and notes on each of the
eight areas on the worksheet. In addition, they are to
think of anything else that has had an effect on their
spiritual journey. The real object of this assignment is
to give them material to share.

My Spiritual Autobiography
Follow the eight steps below to trace your spiritual journey—the history of your relationship with
God. You only have a few minutes, so don't worry
about writing complete sentences. Just get enough
down on paper so that you can share your faith
journey with the other members of your group. Feel
free to use anything that came to mind during the

guided fantasy.

Write down anything you think is relevant, but be sure to include the following items:

1. My earliest memory or awareness of God_____

_____

2. The major religious events or experiences in my life (family, church, youth group, camp, etc.)_____

_____

3. My spiritual high point (when I felt the closest to God) _____

_____

4. My spiritual low point (when I felt most distant from God) _____

_____

5. Special people who have played a role in my faith journey_____

_____

6. Where I am right now in my relationship with God_____

_____

7. Where I would like to be in my relationship with God_____

_____

8. What's missing in my relationship with God_____

_____

Call time at the end of 15 minutes even if the members are not finished. It is important to have plenty of time for sharing. Members can fill in verbally what they did not have time to write.

Share the Spiritual Autobiographies (1 hour). Have each person share his or her spiritual autobiography. Facilitate the discussion by going first, then asking for volunteers. After each person shares, open the group for questions, comments and sharing. Be alert for times when one member's story touches the other members' stories. Continue the process until everyone has had an opportunity to share.

After hearing all the stories, initiate a discussion on insights or comments on the autobiographies as a whole.

If you have a group that shares easily, use time in the second session to finish this exercise.

The Idea of Spiritual Growth (15 minutes). In this exercise, you'll begin teaching about spiritual growth and introduce the concept of spiritual disciplines. Present the following in your own words:

● Spiritual growth is the concept that you can grow closer in your relationship with God and can become closer to God than you now are.

● For centuries, Christians have used specific tools to develop and grow in their relationship with God. These are called spiritual disciplines or spiritual exercises. These spiritual disciplines can be paralleled with other disciplines you are familiar with—athletics, music or study—in any area of life in which you want to grow and become stronger.

● The idea of spiritual growth and spiritual disciplines may be new to some of you, but you already are familiar with many of the disciplines. We have just used two: guided fantasy using scripture and group sharing.

● How many other spiritual disciplines can you come up with? Some ideas include: prayer, meditation, fasting, Bible study, confession, worship, journaling, solitude, service and guidance.

We will be using and experiencing all of these—and more—this weekend.

Are there any questions?

Prayer Journal Assignment (5 minutes). Introduce the idea of a prayer journal: a diary of one's relationship with God and one's spiritual life. Underscore the importance of solitude—a time to be alone with God away from all distractions. Explain that during the periods of solitude, the youth can focus their attention on God through the use of the prayer journals.

Explain that during the journaling time they will be able to think about their relationship with God, pray to God (on paper), and, most importantly, to begin to listen to God.

Say that the journal assignments will be an important part of the weekend. Inform them that the results of the exercises will be shared in the small group sessions.

Ask the students to turn in their booklets to "Prayer Journal—Assignment One" (see below.)

Read aloud the definition of a prayer journal, as it is written on the page. Have the youth work alone on this assignment.

Prayer Journal—Assignment One

1. What is a "prayer journal"?

Read the following quotation that describes what a prayer journal is:

A journal is a personal record of feelings, thoughts, concerns and visions, often written as letters to God. Journal writing is a way of capturing the inner person to gain self-understanding. It includes any and every part of life, but is more concerned with meaning than with events, especially ultimate meaning.

All writing is just talking, put on paper. Many times we are not sure what we think until we say it. When our thoughts, and especially our feelings, reveal our inner selves it is harder to own them, to say them even to a close friend. This is where a

*journal comes in. It is a safe place to face the parts
of ourselves that we don't share anywhere else.*

*Writing in a journal or keeping a journal is a
method that facilitates my taking time and effort to
be honest with myself before God . . .*

*Writing in my journal is a prayer form for me.
"Prayer becomes attention to presence—not only
God's, but our own . . . The transcendent, which
we so neglect and for which we have such deep
yearning, is not only where God lives, but where
we live when are most alive.*[3]

Is there anything that stands out in this quotation and speaks to you personally? If there is, write
it below. Then make some notes about why this is
important to you. _____

_____

_____

If anything is unclear, make a note so that you
can bring it up in your next Spiritual Family Session.

_____

_____

2. A letter to God.

Review your spiritual autobiography; focus on
the parts in which you shared where you are *now*
in your relationship with God, where you would
like to be, and *what's missing* in that relationship.
Add what you hope you can get here this weekend.

Write a prayer in the form of a letter to God.
Talk to God about what you discovered in the form
of a letter to God. Talk to God about what you dis-

---

[3]Louise, C. Spiker, **No Instant Grapes in God's Vineyard** (Valley Forge, PA: Judson,
1982), pp.49-50.

covered as you did your autobiography and re-
viewed the questions. Talk to God as you would
any close friend:

Dear Lord,

3. **A conversation with Jesus.**
   Read the following conversation with Jesus, writ-
ten by Louise Spiker, **No Instant Grapes in God's
Vineyard**, p. 56.

Me: *My trust level isn't very high. I want
signs, like the Old Testament people.*

Jesus: *Now, Louise, I want to help. What exactly
is troubling you? Tell me about it.*

Me: *I'm not sure. I don't feel as okay as I
want to . . . I want to feel good, feel close to
you, to feel some assurance that I'm on
the right track. I'm tense and beginning to
get a headache, but I came to the shore to
get in touch with you and find peace and
power (maybe) and direction. I don't
know, Jesus, I just feel all mixed up.*

Jesus: *You're okay, Louise. You don't have to be
perfect. You don't have to 'arrive' at any
certain place. It's okay to be where you
are now. I love you, Louise. I love and accept you here, now, always. Rest in my
love, Louise.*

Me: *Thank you, Jesus. I want to do that. How about if I just relax here on the beach and feel the sun as your love penetrating to the innermost parts of me?*

Jesus: *I think that's a good idea, Louise. Try it.*

Go back and reread your letter to God. Write a dialogue (like the one above) in which you share your biggest concern in the letter and have Jesus respond. If you experience difficulty having Jesus respond, talk a few moments in silence and see if some reply comes—something that Jesus or God might say.

Me:

Jesus:

Me:

Jesus:

Me:

Jesus:

4. Read John 3:1-21.
Read the passage again and place yourself in the story. You become Nicodemus. You have the conversation with Jesus. Journal on the back of this

page what you hear Jesus saying to you. Write a
dialogue with Jesus if you wish. When you've finished, close with a silent prayer.

Closing Prayer Circle (10 minutes). Have the group
members stand in a circle with their arms around each
other. Begin by singing "Kum Ba Yah."[4] Suggested
verses are: Thank you, Jesus; We love you, Lord;
Come by here, my Lord.

Beginning with the person on your right. Ask him or
her to say a prayer remembering the needs, pains and
joys heard during the session. Go around the circle and
have each youth participate.

Close the prayer yourself. Then lead the group in the
prayer of St. Francis by lining it out—you first say each
line, and the group repeats after you.

The Prayer of St. Francis

Lord,
  make me an instrument of your peace:
    where there is hatred,
      let me sow love;
    where there is injury,
      pardon;
    where there is doubt,
      faith;
    where there is darkness,
      light;
    where there is sadness,
      joy.

O Divine Master,
  grant that I may not so much seek
    to be consoled

[4]Songs, p. 11.

as to console,
to be understood
as to understand,
to be loved
as to love;
for it is in giving
that we receive,
it is in pardoning
that we are pardoned,
and it is in dying
that we are born to eternal life.

Amen.

End with a group hug followed with individual hugs.
Break (45 minutes).
Worship (30 minutes). Open with a song such as
"Come to the Water."[5] Build the worship around the
scriptures used during the last session and the theme,
"Is Something Missing?" Ask one or two students to
share their spiritual autobiographies and what they
learned from the experience. Allow one or two more
youth to share insights from the guided fantasy. Close
with a song such as "Jesus Name Above All Names."[6]

SATURDAY
Listening to God Through Devotional Bible Study
Breakfast (45 minutes).
Worship (30 minutes). Open with a song such as
"He's Everything to Me."[7] Discuss the idea of solitude:
being alone, listening to God. Tell the students they will
have an opportunity for 45 minutes of solitude after the

---

[5]**Songs**, p. 171.
[6]Ibid., p. 63.
[7]Ibid., p. 12.

worship. Say that they can work on their prayer journal assignment of just listen and relax. Close with the song "Humble Yourself."[8]

Solitude (45 minutes).

Community Experience

Relaxation Exercises (5 minutes). Use exercises such as toe touches, stretches and deep breathing.

Guided Fantasy (25 minutes). Lead the youth on a guided fantasy based on John 3:1-21.

Retell the Nicodemus story. Ask the youth to imagine they are Nicodemus. Slowly read the following material:

"I am Nicodemus; I seek Jesus out by night. Why am I seeking Jesus? What questions do I have of him? What am I looking for? Why come by night? Who do I not want to see me? Am I ashamed? embarrassed?

"I meet Jesus. What does he look like? Does he welcome me? What do I feel in his presence?

"Jesus makes a puzzling statement, 'Unless you change, you cannot enter my kingdom.' Born again? How? That's impossible. Why does he say this to me? What is he really trying to say? What do I need to change in my life? How should I be different?

"Jesus talks about two kinds of life. What in my life is worldly? What in my life is spiritual? How can I believe in what I've not seen?

"God loves me so much, he sent his Son. For me? What is Jesus offering me? What am I missing? What is God telling me? How can Jesus make a difference in my life?"

Spiritual Family Session

Share Reactions (30 minutes). Discuss the guided fantasy. You've just come out of an experience that was new for many of your group members. Begin your Spir-

---

[8]Songs, p. 14.

itual Family Session by inviting the group to share its experience, feelings, reactions and insights to the fantasy.

What was it like? weird? nice? helpful? Explain.

Have the group members compare the experience to the way they normally use the Bible. What's the difference? Which do they prefer? Do they usually read the Bible with the expectation that God will actually "speak" to them? Is that a new idea for anyone? What do they think about reading the Bible in this way?

Explain that a guided fantasy is one form of a "devotional Bible study"—reading the Bible in such a way that you *expect* God to speak *to you* personally through the story.

Tell your group members that they are going to experience another guided fantasy, one in which Jesus would offer them something that could change their lives.

Guided Fantasy (15 minutes). Ask three young people to read John 4:1-26; 6:26-27, 34-35. Invite the group members to get comfortable, either in their chairs or on the floor.

Read the following meditation slowly. Feel free to change or adapt it as you wish. Use the ellipses (. . .) for pauses to let your group members' imaginations go to work.

"Feel yourself falling . . . falling back through time . . . further . . . to a far distant land long ago . . . You're looking out your window . . . It's hot . . . You see people . . . slowly walking in the dust of the street . . . You're thirsty . . . You go over to the water bucket for a drink . . . but it's empty . . . You decide to go down to the well outside town and get some water and bring it back . . . You leave your home . . . step out into the street . . . feel the heat . . . hear the noise of the people around you . . . What are they saying? . . . hear the sounds of animals . . . Which one's can you hear? . . . Can you see them?

. . . You can smell someone cooking lunch . . . What are
they cooking? . . . Someone is arguing inside a home as
you walk by . . . What are they arguing about? . . .
You're now outside the town, headed for the well . . .
You hear birds singing . . . It's so hot . . . You're thirsty
. . . You look up, and there is someone sitting at the well
. . . a stranger . . . He looks tired . . . and thirsty . . .
He's . . . Jewish!!! . . . Your people and his people have
hated each other for centuries . . . Feel the anger inside
you . . . What's he doing here in your country? . . . Is he
dangerous? . . . Do you feel fear? . . . He doesn't look
dangerous . . . You know he hates you . . . All Jews hate
your people, they always have . . . He's saying something to you . . . He wants you to get him a bucket of
water . . . You have a bucket and he doesn't . . . 'What!
You, a Jew, ask me, a Samaritan, for a drink?' . . . Before you realize it, those words have slipped out . . .
Strange, he doesn't seem mad, he's smiling . . . Now
he's speaking to you again . . . 'If you only knew what
God is offering you right now, you'd be asking me for a
drink . . . a drink of what I can offer you . . . a drink of
living water' . . . You find yourself wondering, 'What's
water got to do with God' . . . God offering me something right now? . . . What *is* living water? . . . and who
is this guy? . . . Must be a joke . . . some kind of wise
guy . . . talking about "living water" and doesn't even
have his own bucket . . . He's speaking again . . . 'Whoever drinks from this well will get thirsty again, but
anyone who drinks what I have to give will never be
thirsty again . . . What I have to give is eternal life' . . .
What kind of water is that? . . . To *never* be thirsty
again . . . To never feel empty (and at times I feel so
empty) . . . To be satisfied . . . at peace . . . You hear
yourself asking for some of this special water . . . he
starts speaking to you again . . . You can't believe what
you're hearing! . . . He knows!!! . . . Your deepest, darkest secret . . . He knows!!! . . . How? . . . How does he

know THAT! . . . Who is this man? . . . Is he some kind
of prophet? . . . He's speaking to you again . . . 'You
worship God one way, and I worship God another . . . I
worship the God I know, you worship a God you've
never really known . . . never really experienced . . .
never really loved' . . . How? . . . How does he know
these things about me? . . . He's still speaking . . . 'The
time will come, in fact is here now, when you will no
longer worship God the way you have in the past . . .
No, from now on you will worship him in spirit . . . and
in truth' . . . You find yourself praying . . . 'Oh, God, I
wish it were true . . . Can I really feel close to you . . .
can I be close to you?' . . . Who is this man? . . . You
speak to him . . . 'I know that someday the Messiah, the
Christ, will come . . . We all look forward to that day
when we can really know God and feel close to God' . . .
He speaks to you again . . . 'I, who am speaking to you, I
am he' . . . (long pause) . . . 'I am the bread of life. Whoever comes to me will never be hungry. Whoever believes in me will never thirst' . . . you look into his eyes
. . . You know the hunger in your life . . . the emptiness
. . . You know what you thirst for . . . and he is offering
it to you . . . right now . . . (long pause) . . .

"Take a moment to bring yourself back into this gathering. When you are ready, come back to our group
circle."

Discuss Guided Fantasy (30 minutes). Initiate a group
discussion on the experience. Focus on some of the following questions:

● How did the use of the five senses at the beginning
help you get into the story, make it more real?

● What was it like to place yourself in the story?

● What was it like to meet Jesus?

● Could you clearly identify your deepest, darkest
secret? What is it like to think Jesus knows even that
about you?

● What does "living water" mean to you? What do
you think God is offering now, here this weekend? Are
you beginning to get an idea of what you can get in
your relationship with God that you didn't have?

Discuss Prayer Journal (30 minutes). Ask the youth if
they understand a "prayer journal." Did the quotation
they were given in the first session help? What do they
think about the idea of a prayer journal? Have any of
the group members journalized in the past? If so, have
them explain.

Were the group members able to write letters to
God? Was it difficult to do this? Explain. Ask if anyone
will share his or her letter. Break the ice by sharing
your own letter.

Probe to find how the group felt about moving beyond
writing a letter to God to actually entering into a conversation with God. What was that like? What's it like
to think of God "speaking" to you? Does it feel awkward to "listen" to God?

Would anyone be willing to share his or her "conversation"? You can facilitate this by going first in sharing
your dialogue.

Prayer Journal Assignment (5 minutes). Go over the
second assignment for the prayer journal (see below).
Ask if there are any questions.

Prayer Journal—Assignment Two

1. **Take a few moments to center yourself—**
experience solitude, enjoy being alone. When
you're ready, do the following exercise.

2. **Read John 2:13-16.**

Read the passage over again using each of your
senses. If you had been there, what would you
have seen? heard? smelled? felt? tasted? Place
yourself in the story. Where would you have been?
Who would you have been? What would you have

felt? done? Journal the results of your meditations
below._____
_____
_____
_____

Use the temple as an image for your life. What's
there that shouldn't be? What clutters up your life
and keeps you from what's really important? What
in your life do you think would really offend Jesus?
Identify as many things as possible and use the space
below to journal them. _____
_____
_____
_____

3. **Journal a prayer to God.** Lifting up the clutter
you see that keeps you from having the kind of relationship with God you would like to have.

Dear Lord,

4. **Concentrate.** Close your eyes, center yourself,
and mentally go over what you've written. Use a
period of silence to see if you can "hear" God
speak to you about what bothers you. If that's difficult, try journaling a conversation with God about
the clutter in your life.

Me:

Jesus:

Me:

Jesus:

Me:

Jesus:

Me:

Jesus:

5. **Close with a silent prayer.**

Closing Prayer (10 minutes). Stand in a circle. Ask
for favorite songs, then sing one or two. Go around the
circle in prayer with each member lifting up the concerns, joys or sorrows other members shared during the
session. Close the prayer yourself.

End with a group hug and individual hugs.

Lunch (1 hour).

Recreation (1 hour and 45 minutes).

Worship (30 minutes). Open with a song such as

"Sing Alleluia to the Lord."[9] Build the service on the scripture used in the session and the theme, "Listening to God Through Devotional Bible Study." Allow a few participants to share reactions to the guided fantasy and the first prayer journal assignment. Close with a song such as "Listen to My Heart Song."[10]

Solitude (1 hour and 30 minutes).
Free Time (1 hour).
Supper (30 minutes).

SATURDAY EVENING

Listening to God Through Prayer

Breathing Exercise (5 minutes). Lead the group in slow, deep breathing. Have the group try a "breath scripture": "Be still (inhale) and know (exhale) that I (inhale) am God (exhale)."

Broadening Traditional Forms of Prayer (10 minutes). Introduce the following traditional forms of prayer and allow time for the students to imagine . . .

● Praise and thanksgiving: Feel God's love, God's joy . . . Give thanks to God for . . .

● Confession and pardon: Measure your life by what God would like you to be . . . Where are disappointments? . . . Feel God's sadness . . . Lift these to the Lord . . . Receive God's forgiveness . . . Feel God's forgiveness enter you . . . Imagine God hugging you . . . Imagine love flowing through your veins . . .

● Petition: Ask for God's help in some area of your life . . . Imagine God's love embracing you without words . . . Feel God's strength and power flowing into you . . . Feel your problem growing smaller, God's power growing stronger . . .

● Intercession: Think of someone in your group or at home who has a problem . . . Ask God's help for that

[9]**Songs**, p. 10.
[10]Ibid., inside front cover.

person . . . Image God's love embracing him or her . . . Image God's power and strength flowing into that person . . . Image his or her problem or pain growing weaker as the power of God grows . . .

New Ways to Pray (15 minutes). Introduce the following new ways to pray. Allow time for the students to imagine . . .

● Centering prayer: Focus on the center of your body . . . Release tension, be at peace . . . Feel peace flow out from your center . . .

● Emptying prayer (kenosis—one form of contemplation): Relax, release tension . . . Remove everything from awareness . . . Be empty, silent . . . Dwell in empty silence . . . Listen to silence . . . ½lsten to God . . .

● Jesus prayer: "Lord Jesus, have mercy upon me, a sinner" . . . Repeat this over and over in your mind until the prayer is all that exists . . .

● Scripture prayer (meditation): "I have come that you might have life and have it abundantly" . . . Repeat the verse over and over in your mind . . . See if any word stands out, if any images or thoughts come . . . Let your imagination go . . . Go with whatever comes into your mind . . .

● Mantra: Lift up one word in your mind such as life, love, peace, joy . . . Repeat the word over and over in your mind . . . Begin to feel what the word means . . . Feel life, love, peace, joy . . . Dwell in the feeling . . . Let it flow over you . . . into you . . . through you . . .

Spiritual Family Session

Discuss Reactions to Exercises (15 minutes). Begin the session by having the group members share their experiences and reactions to the prayer exercises. Incorporate the following questions:

Which of the exercises were new to you? Which did you find difficult to get into? Which did you enjoy or find particularly helpful? Explain. Which was the most vivid or powerful? How does this way of praying compare with the way you usually pray? What do you think about this approach? Which of these could you use in your own prayer life? Share your reactions, thoughts or feelings to prayer as *listening to God* rather than telling God something.

The Importance of Listening (15 minutes). Ask the group to discuss what it takes to make a good friend. What do they look for in a good friendship? What does it take to *maintain* a good friendship?

Once the group has a good idea of what friendship is and what it needs, ask what the group thinks about the following three qualities in a friendship:

- time together
- quality time (away from all distractions)
- listening

Ask the group members to think about their relationship with God as an intimate friendship. Ask what they can lift up from the discussion on friendship and apply to their relationship with God. Do we nurture our friendship with God? Do we take time with God? Do we have quality time away from all distractions? Do we ever listen to God really expecting that God can speak to us? What kind of clutter do we allow to get in the way of our friendship with God?

Discuss Prayer Journal (15 minutes). Have the group members share their journaling experiences. Were they able to use the devotional Bible study techniques to make the scripture more real? What happened when they placed themselves in the story? What "clutter" were they able to identify? (What gets in the way of their friendship with God?) Could they identify anything they feel might offend Jesus?

Cleansing the Temple (1 hour). Explain that one of the primary goals of the spiritual disciplines is to create a place in our lives where God can speak to us, to remove all the clutter—all the conflicting claims on our time and our energy—so that we make room and time to be with God

Four of the spiritual disciplines are specifically intended to remove clutter, the noises and distractions that keep us from listening to God. As you go over these four disciplines below, the idea is to find if any of these could be useful in getting rid of some of the distracting clutter that we have identified. (The goal is to initiate sharing and discussion.)

● **Solitude.** Share the following definition of solitude with the group: "Solitude, as a spiritual discipline, means to spend time alone, in silence, listening to God. It is a deliberate stepping back from all the activities, people, distractions and noise of our normal day, so that we can spend some quality time with God."[11]

Your group has now had two opportunities for solitude this weekend. Ask the group members to share what those experiences were like.

Ask if anyone experiences solitude at home—being totally alone, in silence (no stereo, radio or television). What's that experience like at home? Could the experience be negative (lonely)?

What regular times of solitude would add to your relationship with God that is not already there? What clutter might it remove?

● **Fasting.** Ask what fasting means. Then share the following definition: "Fasting, as a spiritual discipline, means to abstain from food for a set period of time for spiritual purposes—not to lose weight or to make a political point (as in a hunger strike). The spiritual purpose of fasting is to heighten awareness of God's presence and to free us from a preoccupation with food."[12]

To better understand how fasting can heighten awareness, ask if any youth have ever eaten so much

---

[11]Paraphrased from Richard Foster, **Celebration of Discipline: Paths to Spiritual Growth** (San Francisco: Harper & Row, 1978).

[12]Ibid.

that they become sleepy or sluggish. Explain that not eating, especially for a long period of time, can do the opposite—it can make a person more alert and aware

Ask if anyone in the group has ever fasted. If so, discuss the experience. Encourage the group to ask questions of those who have fasted.

If no one in the group has fasted, you might share some of the following information:

Those who do fast say that it can make us more alert and aware of things around us and within us, including God's presence. People who fast find that after 24 to 48 hours of fasting, it is much easier to pray. Fasting also can free us from a preoccupation with food. Most of us spend a good amount of our time either eating, talking about food, preparing food or thinking about food. It consumes a lot of our time and energy. Many people are surprised to discover that they don't need to eat three times a day. After a day or so, the person who is fasting may not even be hungry, and may even find his or her energy level has increased.

Initiate a discussion on fasting. What are fears and myths about fasting? Is it a spiritual discipline the youth might like to try?

● **Simplicity.** Read the following quotation from **Celebration of Discipline: Paths to Spiritual Growth,** by Richard Foster:

Simplicity is freedom . . . Because we lack a divine Center our need for security has led us into an insane attachment to things. We must clearly understand that the lust for affluence in contemporary society is psychotic. It is completely psychotic because it has completely lost touch with reality. We crave things we neither need nor enjoy. We buy things we do not want to impress people we do not like . . . We are made to feel ashamed to wear clothes or drive cars until they are worn out. The

*mass media have convinced us that to be out of
step with fashion is to be out of step with
reality.*[13]

Ask if Foster is overstating the case. Is happiness to
be found in more and more "things"? If we have
enough, own enough, possess enough, if there is enough
money in our bank account, will we be happy? Get the
group to think about this for a few minutes.

As a spiritual discipline, simplicity affirms that more
"things" cannot make us happy. In fact, possessions
can clutter up our life and lead us away from what's
really important. In our society, many believe that the
importance or worth of a person is measured by the
wealth or the amount of possessions. The discipline of
simplicity says that this is not true.

Ask if the group can identify ways in which the "lust
for affluence" makes a relationship with other people
and with God more difficult. Do they experience this in
their school? churches? families? Where else?

How could this discipline help their personal relationship with God? What clutter could it remove from their
lives?

● **Submission.** Read the following definition of submission: "Another word for submission is "servanthood." As a spiritual discipline, submission affirms that
the way to self-fulfillment is through self-denial—to
hold other's interests above self-interest."[14]

Initiate a discussion on this definition. Is the idea of-
fensive? naive?

After everyone has had an opportunity to react to the
definition, ask if anyone has ever encountered a person
who seemed totally absorbed with himself or herself.
Have them discuss their reactions.

---

[13]Foster, **Celebration of Discipline: Paths to Spiritual Growth**, pp. 69-79.
[14]Ibid., paraphrased.

Have the youth ever known of someone who seemed to value them as much as they did themselves? If they have, have them discuss their reactions. If not, have them fantasize what it might be like to know such a person.

Encourage the youth to consider the idea of a group—like your group—in which everyone is more concerned about each other than about themselves.

How could the discipline of submission help their relationship with God? What clutter could it help remove?

Prayer Journal Assignment (5 minutes). Ask the students to turn to their booklets to the third prayer journal assignment (see below). Ask if there are any questions.

Prayer Journal—Assignment Three

1. **Reflect and meditate.** How has God come to you through other people? How have people been important in your faith journey? Go back to your autobiography. Who has helped you? Name specific people, events and experiences. What was it about these persons that made them instruments of God in your life? Were they special in any way? Journal what you uncover._____

_____

_____

_____

2. **Review the weekend so far.** Who has God used for you this weekend? How has God used them? Do you think God has used you this weekend to help anyone else? Write your answers in the space below._____

_____

_____

_____

3. **Read 1 Corinthians 12:12-30.**
How has God used "the body" (the church, your youth group, camp, individual Christians) in your life?_____
_____
_____
_____

How has God used you to help others? _____
_____
_____
_____

4. **Write a prayer letter to God.** Lift up what you've discovered during this assignment.

Dear Lord,

5. **Close with a silent prayer.**

Closing Prayer (10 minutes). Stand in a prayer circle. Sing a song such as "We Are the Family of God."[15]
Go around the circle in a prayer having each member lift the concerns heard during the session. Close the prayer yourself.

---

[15]**Songs**, p. 65.

End with a group hug and individual hugs.

Dance (2 hours and 45 minutes). Everyone should be in their rooms by midnight with lights out at 1 a.m.

SUNDAY MORNING

Listening to God Within "The Body"
Breakfast, Pack, Load (1 hour).
Solitude (30 minutes).

Community Experience

Relaxation and Guided Fantasy (30 minutes). Have the youth lie on the floor so that everyone is both supporting and supported by others. Slowly read John 15:1-8. Take the youth on a guided fantasy:

"Imagine yourself as the branch. You are drawing nourishment and strength from God (the vine) . . . Feel the strength flowing in . . . flowing into your feet . . . up through your body . . . out of your arms and head . . . flowing into you, through you, to others around you . . . You're being supported by other branches around you . . . by the bodies you are lying on . . . You are not alone . . . You are surrounded, supported . . . Feel that support . . . Feel strength, nourishment flowing into you from those around you . . . Feel the connection between you and everyone else here . . . all a part of the vine . . . God's strength flowing into you from others . . . flowing to others from you . . ."

Have the youth keep their eyes closed as you read 1 Corinthians 12:12-30. Take the youth on a second guided fantasy:

"Imagine yourself as one small part of a body . . . Feel the other parts of the body around you . . . so small, dependent on the other parts . . . for nourishment . . . for help . . . for life . . . You can't say to others, 'I don't need you' . . . Cut off from others, you would die . . . so small, yet important . . . You have your part to do . . . Without you the work would not get done . . . Feel the others who rest on you . . . depend on you for support . . . No one can say to you, 'I don't need you' . . . Without you the body would not be whole . . . Feel a sense of belonging . . . You are a part of the body . . . Feel your place, how you are connected to all around you . . ."

Spiritual Family Session

Discussion (20 minutes). Have the group process the two guided fantasies.

● The vine: What was it like to be a part of the vine? Could you feel the strength flowing into you? Does that ever really happen to you? Explain. What was it like to feel yourself supported by others? Where do you get that in real life? at home? in school? at church? in youth group? here? Have you ever felt cut off from the vine and the other branches? What was that like? How important is being a part of the vine to you personally? Could you be more attached than you are, more supported?

● The body: Compare "the body" exercise with "the vine." How were they different? similar? What's it like to have to depend on others? What's it like to have others depend on you? Are you needed? important? Do you have a contribution to make?

Discuss Prayer Journal (10 minutes). Have the group members share how God has come to them in other people in the past. Guide the sharing with the following questions: What did these people do? How are these people different from others? Do you think God has ever used you in someone else's life? Has God worked through anyone this weekend? (Use these questions to set up the next exercise.)

Spiritual Healing Exercise (30 minutes). Have the group members sit in a circle on the floor. Ask for a volunteer. The volunteer is to share one hurt or need he or she has. The rest of the group is to try to listen and understand that hurt. The youth cannot give advice or try to "solve" the problem. They can ask questions to try to understand the problem better, and they can share their concerns. When the person feels the group has heard and understands his or her problem, he or she should lie down in the middle of the circle while everyone else places one hand on him or her. Each person in the group then gives a verbal prayer for the person in the center. The prayer lifts up the pain or problem and asks for healing. When the prayer is finished, have the person in the center share the experience. Repeat the process with other volunteers.

Prayer Journal Assignment (5 minutes). Ask the students to turn in their booklets to the fourth prayer journal assignment (see below). Ask if there are any questions.

Prayer Journal—Assignment Four
1. **Read John 21:15-17.**
Identify someone in your church youth group that you know needs help and support. Be very specific. What does the person need? _____

_____

_____

_____

_____

Identify someone at camp (who is not in your group) who needs help and support. _____

_____

_____

_____

_____

Write how you could help meet this need before

leaving today. Be aware that you will be given an
opportunity to reach out to these two people during
the closing worship service. _____

_____

_____

_____

    2. **Review the weekend**—all you have learned
and experienced. In the space below, write what
you will take with you from this weekend and use
at home in your spiritual journey. Note any commitments you've made._____

_____

_____

_____

    Closing Prayer (10 minutes). Have the group get into
a circle and begin with a song such as "Jesus My
Lord."[16]
Join in a prayer circle giving thanks for the weekend.
Close the prayer yourself and lead the group in the
Lord's Prayer.
    Close with a group hug and individual hugs.
    Solitude (15 minutes). Have the youth complete the
fourth prayer journal assignment.
    Closing Worship (30 minutes). Open with a song such
as "Just a Closer Walk."[17] Build the service on any
scripture used the past weekend and the theme "Spiritual Growth—Reaching Out." Allow time for the students to reach out to the two people they identified in
their fourth prayer journal assignment. Close with several of the songs that were sung during the retreat.

[16]**Songs**, p. 14.
[17]Ibid., p. 40.

10

Spiritual and Physical Fitness

As we think about a "wholistic" or whole-person approach to ministry, we think about getting our head and heart together, but we sometimes forget about our body. In order to feel good about others, we first must feel good about ourselves. In order to feel good about ourselves, we need to be in good physical and spiritual condition.

The notion that our bodies need proper nourishment and care has been vaulted into prominence with the advent of the emphasis on running and exercise. Aerobics has become a great part of Americans' leisure time. Some church leaders have moved in the direction of aerobics for Christians. They combine aerobics with Christian music and choose names for their aerobic classes such as "Devotion in Motion" and "Youth Aerobics."

A consistent exercise program is one way to get into good physical condition. A consistent spiritual discipline program is a good way to get into good spiritual condition. In this chapter, I will describe a model which combines physical and spiritual exercises.

The idea of using exercise, flexibility, stretching and body awareness along with spiritual meditation is not new. This concept has been used throughout the ages in both Eastern and Western civilizations. The care of the body is definitely a spiritual matter: "Do you not know that your body is a temple of the Holy Spirit within you, which you have from God? You are not your own; you were bought with a price. So glorify God in your body" (1 Corinthians 6:19-20).

Rose Mary Miller, associate director of Youth Ministries Consultation Service, has combined the aerobic movement with music and spiritual meditation. The following is an example of one of Rose Mary's programs. This model has been used very effectively at the beginning of a retreat or gathering when everyone is full of energy and excited about being together. This program offers a way to wind down, center on one's self and open communication with God. You will need:

● One cassette player with good quality sound.

● One cassette tape with soft, quiet meditative music. For example: "Father's Eyes," by Amy Grant; "We Are the Reason," by David Meece; "In This Very Room," by Free Spirit. Lionel Richie and George Benson also have some beautiful songs you could use.

● One cassette with fast music or an exercise tape. Carol Hensel's Exercise and Dance program comes with a booklet describing some exercises which are good for beginners and are easy to follow. Most exercise tapes come with instructions.

● One exercise mat for each person or a large area of carpet for the entire class.

If you have never participated in an aerobics class

and would be uncomfortable leading a program, recruit someone to help you. This program is an excellent opportunity to involve new individuals in your youth program. Chances are that someone in your church is taking an aerobics class and would be glad to help lead the group. Some high schools offer aerobics in their physical education classes. Ask one of your youth to lead the exercises or call your local health club and invite an aerobics teacher to lead the class.

1. **Warm up (5 to 10 minutes).** Ask everyone to take an exercise mat and find a place on the floor. Begin the program by playing some soft music.

Explain that this is not a full aerobics class, it is just an opportunity to wake up the senses—to loosen up, concentrate and communicate with God. Explain to the youth that you will begin by leading slow stretches to warm up their muscles, then you will continue with flexibility and endurance exercises to faster music.

More than likely, several of your youth are not in a regular exercise program. Tell the youth: "We are all at different levels in our flexibility and endurance; so if you get tired, slow down and do only the exercises that are comfortable for you. None of these exercises should be painful. If it hurts, your body is trying to tell you to slow down."

Lead the participants in the following stretches:

"Stand with your knees slightly bent, shoulder width apart. Stretch and flex your fingers and slowly reach up to the ceiling. Drop your arms and relax.

"Take a few slow, deep breaths. Breathe in through your nose and out through your mouth.

"Keep your knees slightly bent. Now, do a curl down. Slowly drop your chin to your chest. Keep curling down. one vertebra at a time until your hands reach your knees. Reach up to the ceiling and stretch your fingers once again.

"Repeat the curl down. This time, slowly curl down

until your hands reach the floor. Reach to the ceiling and stretch your fingers one last time.

"Straighten your legs as much as you can without hurting. Take one more slow, deep breath—in through your nose, out through your mouth."

2. **Exercise (5 to 10 minutes).** Play the exercise tape or put on some popular fast music. You or your recruited teachers can lead the class in exercises. Another option is to divide into small groups and let each group choose a leader. Ask the leaders to make up their own dance steps and exercises to the music. Some examples of endurance exercises are: jogging in place, walking briskly, jumping jacks and high kicks.

3. **Cool down (5 to 10 minutes).** Play the cassette with quiet, meditative music and slowly stretch out with some of the same exercises you used in the beginning warm up.

4. **Meditate (5 minutes).** After the cool down and everyone's breathing is back to normal, ask the youth to find their own space on the floor. Note that they should have enough room so as not to touch anyone. Slowly guide the students in the following meditation:

"Lay down and close your eyes. If you are wearing glasses, you may want to take them off. Relax. Press the arch out of your back and tuck your shoulder blades under so that you are comfortable. Take a slow, deep breath—in through your nose and out through your mouth. Do this three times. Take the palms of your hands and in a circular motion gently massage your temples. Next, take your thumbs and in a circular motion gently massage beneath your eyebrows and across the top of your eyes. Now, take your fingertips and gently massage along the back of your neck and along the top of your shoulders. Relax your arms down to the floor. Take a deep breath—in through your nose and out through your mouth. Lift your right arm slightly off the floor and stretch as hard as you can. Stretch the fingers in your right arm ... stretch ... now, let your arm drop and totally relax. Relax the fingers in your right hand ... your right forearm ... your right arm is totally relaxed. Feel the difference in your right arm and your left arm. Now, lift your left arm just slightly off the floor and stretch ... (Follow this same relaxation technique with the left arm, right leg and the left leg.) Take a slow, deep breath—in through your nose and out through your mouth. (At this point, everyone will be relaxed and every eye should be closed.) Be aware of your heart beat. Be aware of your breathing ... 'In the beginning God created the heavens and the earth. The earth was without form and void, and darkness was upon the face of the deep; and the Spirit of God was moving over the face of the waters.' Take in the breath of God ... let it out slowly ... relax and feel all the tension and stress of the day flow out of your fingertips. (Pause for a few moments of silence.) This is what I call my 'listen-to-God time.' I've found often in my prayer life I was doing a lot of talking and never any listening. I would like to invite you for the next few times to use this as your 'listen-to-God time.' Just relax and listen ..."

As people begin to stir or open their eyes say, "When you are ready to bring your time with God to a close, you may open your eyes."

When all of the students have opened their eyes, invite them to form a circle. Ask if the students would like to share how they felt or what happened to them during the exercise. Give them time to respond. Tell them that this is an exercise they can do on their own to relax and release tension. You can give a personal example such as, "When I am under pressure to complete a project, I will take 10 minutes to do some relaxation and spend time alone with God. This time gives me enough strength and energy to come back to the project refreshed and ready to move on."

Spiritual growth and physical exercise go together to make us healthy individuals.

A Program for Relational Spiritual Growth

The culmination of your personal and youth group spiritual growth efforts is a spiritual growth program involving both you (the leader) and the youth group. In this 32-week program, make a commitment to pray for, phone, write and visit 40 targeted youth. You can successfully accomplish this goal by setting aside an average of an hour a day for 32 weeks. (For our purposes, we have planned for 40 youth over 32 weeks. You can easily adapt this design to your needs.)

The 32-week program is a good test of your own personal spiritual growth. Furthermore, the program opens up many possibilities such as increased youth attendance and a heightened caring for one another. You will notice a significant change in your attitude about ministry and an increase in your awareness of the individual needs of your youth. The 32-week period allows you enough time set a discipline for yourself and also to check the system for results.

SELECTION OF 40 YOUTH

The 32-week program is not just for the active and inactive members of your group: It includes their friends.

1. **Actives**—young people who attend youth group on a regular basis. They are not just the "core kids," but are youth who are touched in some phase by the youth program such as the "nursing home visiting group," "choir" or "Sunday school."

2. **Inactives**—youth who do not attend youth group, yet are on the roll because their families belong to the church. Inactives could have been active at one time and then replaced youth group with other interests.

3. **Friends of actives and inactives**—acquaintances and friends who probably attended a retreat, party or other youth group program. These youth tend to show up only when something "is happening." They are good prospects for membership.

To select youth for this program, write the names of the actives, inactives and friends on separate 3×5 cards. Make three stacks, separating them according to the categories. On a piece of paper, prepare a copy of the chart on the following page which denotes each area of your experiment: prayer, phone, letter and visit.

Randomly choose a name from each stack of cards and write it in the first column. Continue this process until you have 10 names in each column. By alternating the names from the categories, you will be sure to give the same attention to each category. Later, when this list is mailed to the youth and posted in the youth room, everyone will notice that all participants are treated equally. The following is an example of a completed chart:

Prayer	Phone	Letter	Visit
Ron. (active)	Ralph (inactive)		
Brenda (inactive)	Linda (friend)		
Betty (friend)	Dave (active)		
John (active)	Natalie (inactive)		
Bill (inactive)			
Lois (friend)	etc.		
Sue (active)			
Jerry (inactive)			
Joe (friend)			
Mary (active)			

After a period of eight weeks, you will rotate the names to the next column. For instance, the 10 people you prayed for will be moved to the phone column. The 10 people you phoned will be moved to the letter column, and so on. When the 32-week program is complete, all 40 youth will have received equal amounts of prayer, phone calls, letters and visits.

THE INTRODUCTORY LETTER

After completing this chart, write a letter to each of the 40 youth explaining the 32-week program. It's not necessary that the letter be personalized or individualized. In fact, it is better to write a form letter so that no one has a sense of being singled out.

When writing your letter, tell the youth that you are beginning a new spiritual growth program that involves them. Explain that although their names are on the list, there is no commitment necessary from them. The program is an effort on your part to enhance the spirituality of the youth group as well as yourself. Give a general description of the program and include the chart of the people involved in the experiment. To personalize each letter, handwrite a note at the bottom and explain the aspect of the program in which each youth will be involved for the first eight weeks.

Larry Young of Pearland, Texas, experimented with the 32-week program in his youth group. Here is a copy of the letter he sent out:

November 27

Dear Members and Friends of First Methodist,

I believe that friendships grow only when people make an effort to know each other. I also believe that teenagers and adults can be good friends.

In light of this, I am introducing a program whereby I will seek out 40 teenagers in an effort to promote friendship. You are a part of this program. But do not be alarmed. You will not be asked to make any type of commitment and there is nothing you must do.

You have been randomly placed in a group and, depending upon which group you are in, several things may happen. Over the next eight weeks some of you will be prayed for daily. Others of you will receive a weekly phone call, while some will receive a letter. And still another group of you will be called for an appointment to visit in your home.

At the end of the eight weeks, I will rotate your names so the ones that received prayers will receive phone calls, the ones that received phone calls will receive letters, and so on. At the end of the 32 weeks, all 40 of you will have received an equal number of prayers, phone calls, letters and visits.

I am enclosing a copy of the group in which you are a part. This is for your information so that you will know what to expect. If you have any questions, please feel free to call me.

In Christ's love,

Larry

Larry Young

Dear Jeff, I will be praying for you each day for the next eight weeks. Larry

THE SPIRITUAL PROGRAM BOARD

It is important that the program have high visibility, but not the extent of detracting from the original intent. Many times we become slaves to a program and the people it serves suffer. This happens because we want people to know we're "doing our job."

One way to increase the visibility of the 32-week program is to create a "spiritual program board." On a 4-foot-by-8-foot piece of plywood, paint an enlargement of your chart (see page 196). Each slot should be large enough for a 3×5 card that you prepared earlier (see page 195). Affix a cup hook in each slot. Paper punch a hole on each card and hang the cards on the cup hooks.

Hang the board on a wall in your youth room so the program will be visible to the students throughout the 32 weeks. This board reinforces the attention the youth are receiving from you as well as reminds you to follow through with your commitment to the program.

After each eight-week segment, rotate the name cards to the next column. For instance, move the 10 prayer cards to the phone list, the phone list to the letter list, and so on. This way, the participants will be aware of the aspect they will be involved in over the next eight weeks.

When the 32-week program has been completed, take the board down and store it for later use.

SPECIAL NEEDS BOX

For this 32-week program, prepare a "special needs box" as a means for the youth to tell you their concerns and needs. Although the special needs box is not a new idea, it certainly is a practical, non-threatening way of determining the needs of the group.

To construct this item, cover a shoe box with wrapping paper. Use paint, marker or letters cut out of construction paper to create the label, "Special Needs Box." Cut a 4-inch slot in the top of the box. Reinforce the slot with masking tape. Write the instructions on a posterboard (see illustration below). Attach the instructions to the box. Tie a pencil to the end of a long piece of string, then tape the other end of the string to the posterboard. On top of the box, glue a small note pad. Place the box next to the spiritual program board.

Introduce the concept to the youth and explain that whenever they have needs or concerns, they are encouraged to write these on paper and drop the notes into the box. Emphasize that the notes will be kept confidential. Explain that after each group meeting, you will empty the box and pray for the concerns and needs.

Occasionally, someone may drop a rude or smart-alecky note into the box. Do not get upset and do not acknowledge the note. In the same way, if you take the authentic notes seriously, they not only will continue, but will multiply.

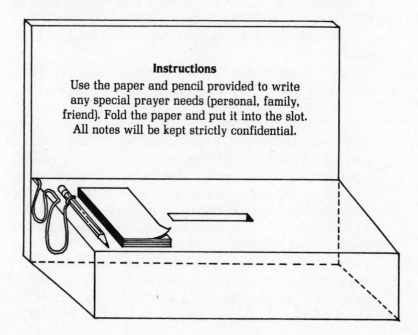

Instructions
Use the paper and pencil provided to write any special prayer needs (personal, family, friend). Fold the paper and put it into the slot. All notes will be kept strictly confidential.

PRAYER

As with all the other aspects of this program, you will devote an equal amount of time praying for each of the 40 youth. When we unselfishly care for others as Christ cares for us, we grow and develop a closer relationship with them and God. This process is designed to promote spirituality as something that is done and not just talked about.

For the prayer aspect of the 32-week program, select the same time every day to pray for the youth on the list. Pray for them by name and need as each group of 10 is rotated into the prayer slot. You can find the needs of these youth by talking with them at youth group, observing them at events, or by reading the notes in the special needs box.

If the youth are inactive or friends of the youth group, you may find it difficult to pray for their needs. Research, then, becomes important. Ask the youth group members about their friends and the inactives or call these people to ask if they have special prayer requests. It is amazing what you can discover when you ask.

When you pray, mention the name of the youth, the need, and pray for your own awareness and sensitivity to that young person. For example:

"Gracious Lord, I lift Ron to you. Ron has seemed so depressed lately. From what I have heard from him, I suspect that his parents are not getting along very well and are taking it out on him. He thinks the safest thing to do is get away from home. I really identify with Ron; I feel as if I have been there. I don't know how to tell him, however, and I'm not sure I should. I don't want to meddle, but I do want to help. Show me the way to "be there" for Ron. Give me the awareness, wisdom and words to say. Teach me patience when Ron is not responding at youth group to know there is some trouble somewhere within him. Help me deal with the problem instead of the symptom. Thank you, Lord.

"I also come to you for Brenda, Lord. Brenda seems to be so enthralled with a senior she is dating; yet she is only 15. I know he's pressing non-Christian values on her but she is so taken in by him. I see a lot of not-so-good signs, but I don't know exactly what to do. Some people have told me, 'It's not your problem!' Others think I ought to talk to her and perhaps her parents. Show me what to do, Lord. I don't want to alienate her, but I don't want her to get hurt either. I need your guidance . . ."

God will hear your prayers. When you see each one of those youth after you have been parying for them, you will have an awareness of and sensitivity for them as people rather than "numbers" in your youth group. Your relationship with them will improve because you will know them better.

One of the greatest rewards from this process is when we discover that youth can minister to us, too. Many times I have had youth come to me and tell me that they have been praying for me. It has been especially affirming to be reminded of the power of prayer. Watch and experience the results.

TELEPHONE

The 10 people on the phone list of the spiritual program board are to be called once a week during the eight-week period. Your only motivation should be to check on them. You should not use the calls for recruiting for a retreat or urging attendance at the youth group.

The youth connection is the telephone. Youth know how to talk on the phone, will talk on the phone, like to receive phone calls, and want and need affirmation. All of these are given aspects about young people, so you can assume that youth will respond if you call.

In your initial check-in call, let the one who is called

take the initiative for conversation. For example, I usually say: "Hi, Mike. This is David. I wrote you that I would be calling you one time each week to just check on you. How are things going?"

Give the youth an opportunity to respond to that statement. Allow conversation to develop on its own. Remember that it is not necessary to hold a lengthy discussion. Conversations will become natural after several calls. Be patient. Do not push. Allow this process to take its own course.

LETTERS

To receive a personal letter, at any age, is exciting and gratifying because of the attention we are given. For people to care enough about us to pause and write is uplifting. This is felt even more strongly by adolescents. With such a large percentage of young people feeling a need to belong and be accepted, a kind word in a letter becomes a prized piece of literature.

I am continually saddened when I go into a young person's room and see a mimeographed letter to "Dear Student" from Junior Achievement hanging on his or her bulletin board. If a young person would keep an impersonal letter like that, think of what a personal letter from you would mean!

Ask five teenagers what they do with personal letters they receive. If more than one says, "I throw them away," write me a letter and set me straight. I know that young people keep those priceless letters.

Schedule a time each week to write your letters. Early in the morning is the best time for me. I keep all of my writing materials together to facilitate the process. One letter a week to each of the 10 youth on the list takes little time and yet means a great deal. I suggest the following formula for your letter writing:

1. Affirmation. The first and fifth letters should be letters of affirmation. It is important to include a few

lines to affirm a quality about the youth or just say
something nice. For example:

Dear Margaret,
    This is just a note to begin our letter-writing pro-
gram the next eight weeks. I am excited to be doing this. You will make it especially easy for me
because there are so many things about you that I
like. You are a valuable asset to our youth group. I
look forward to the coming weeks of getting to
know you better and calling on your gifts to help
out.

In Him, we really are one,

---

2. **Gifts.** The second and sixth letters should recognize the gifts of each youth. Sometimes when we think
of gifts that youth have, we do not look below the sur-
face. We tend to notice only that people are pretty, ath-
letic, popular or a leader. We should not overlook important gifts such as: the ability to make friends, sensitivity to the poor, courage to speak out and other self-
less attitudes. Pointing out that you have noticed special
gifts is rewarding to the youth.
    When you write the letters, state specific rather than
general gifts you have noticed. Instead of saying, "I like
the way you make people feel included" say, "That was
a nice thing you said to Susan last Sunday night when
she was crying."

Dear Bobby,
 I do not believe you! No one else in the entire group has the uncanny ability to size up a situation the way you do and then say the right thing. What a gift! Sunday, when we were bogged down about what to do about the bike hike, your counsel to not make it a race was brilliant! I don't know why I hadn't thought of that sooner. Anyway, thanks for being a friend and a super insightful person!

In Him, we really are one,

3. Accomplishment. The third and seventh letters are in recognition of accomplishment. When we think of accomplishment, usually it pertains to trophies or elections. Think of accomplishment as attaining personal goals. For example:

Dear John,
 Congratulations on getting your driver's license! What a privilege. I know you must be a careful driver because I know of your sensitivity for the well-being of people. I am looking forward to riding with you soon!

Good luck and good driving,

4. Availability. The fourth and eighth letters note your availability to tell people you are available to them without having made an attempt to establish a relationship seems hollow. It is important to build a relationship through the previous letters before writing a letter of availability. This lends credibility to your program. Here is an example of a letter of availability:

> Dear Susan,
> I have enjoyed getting to know you through this letter writing. It is amazing when I sit down and write you how I picture you right here. I just want to say that if you ever need to talk or if I can ever help you out on anything, don't hesitate to give me a call. My office numer is 555-1718 and my home number is 555-2166.
>
> In Him, we really are one,

Sometimes it is difficult to know what to write week in and week out. If this happens, pretend you are talking to the person and write down your thoughts. Reread what you wrote and include the formula material such as affirmation, gifts noticed, accomplishment or availability. Then write your letter according to these thoughts.

VISITATION

"I thought the visiting part of the spiritual program would be the most difficult. Maybe it is, but it is also the most rewarding thing I have ever done in the youth ministry program of our church!" said a youth worker who experimented with this program.

Each of the 10 youth on the visitation list must get one home visit, one school visit, and one social place visit during the eight-week period.

1. The home visit. Make an appointment a week or two in advance. Call the day before to tell the youth you have not forgotten that you have an appointment with him or her. (Notice the positive way of reminding the youth about the appointment.) Keep the appointment. then follow up with a phone call to get any additional information that you need.

Some of the dynamics of a good home visit include:

● Have no agenda except to "get to know the youth better."

● Publicize that you are visiting as a part of a program so they do not think you are singling them out for a visit.

● When you visit, you have the right to "dismiss" brothers, sisters and parents.

● To avoid gossip or accusations, never go into a home where there is no responsible adult.

An alternative to the home visit is to take a walk with the youth, visit on the porch or ask the youth to help run errands with you after school. I seldom recommend that you take a young person to get a cola. The youth may be embarrassed to be with an "older" person in front of his or friends. Exceptions would be if you are already close friends and it feels natural, or if you are close to the young person's age and look the part of a school friend.

2. The school visit. One time during the eight-week period, visit in the school or at a school function such as a talent show or ballgame. To complete the requirement of the school visitation you simply have to be seen on campus. While on campus, you will be able to identify with "Mean Mr. Hanson," "that terrible cafeteria food" or "our great team." The school visit will increase your understanding of the youth culture and bet-

ter your insight for conversations. It is not necessary to
talk with the youth—just be seen.

When you plan a school visit, always secure permission through the principal's office. Work to establish
"common ground" with the principal by talking about
the importance of building relationships with youth or
about the "cost of discipleship" of being a youth
worker. Let the principal know that you are not there to
upset anything by conducting a Bible study or prayer
group. You just want to be there. Ask the principal to
suggest a good time to visit. Almost always, he or she
will suggest that you come at lunch time.

The first time you go to a school, ask a person from
your youth group to meet you. He or she probably will
bring a friend. Where several of you are gathered,
others will join you. If you go alone, members of your
youth group will probably wave to you and even speak,
but not come sit with you. To them, it would be embar-
rassing!

Some schools have had bad experiences with church
or parachurch organizations "pushing" religion. Most
schools now have rules such as, "No one may visit the
school if he or she is representing a church." You could
question the constitutionality of that or visit in other
ways such as volunteering to substitute teach or being
present for ballgames, talent shows, beauty contests or
debate tournaments. Schools are open for your participation in extracurricular activities. One time around in
a gymnasium and you will see many hands waving. We
are talking about visibility!

3. The social visit. During the eight-week period, each
of the 10 people on the visit list also should be visited in
a social setting such as a dance, party, hangout or
restaurant.

Before you can make one of these social visits, do
your "homework." To visit in one of these social situations without first having established a quasi-friendship

or relationship with the youth could prove disastrous to your ego. It is difficult to feel comfortable in a social setting when you do not really know some of the people there. Be sure to work on the relationships at home and school before making this move.

KEEPING RECORDS

Throughout the 32-week program, keep track of your progress by writing down the results of your prayers, phone conversations, letters and visits. It also is a check to be sure you are following through on items that emerge as the program progresses.

Make a copy of the following record page for each of the 40 youth in the program. Use these instructions:

1. **Prayer record.** Record any special notes concerning your prayer time for each youth. What have you done as a result of praying for the needs? What are any significant changes in yourself? the youth?

2. **Phone record.** Each week list the topic conversation. This will help you avoid repeating yourself. It also will trigger your memory for the next conversation.

3. **Letter record.** Include a specific note on "what you said" in each letter. This will help you not to repeat yourself and it also will help to focus the direction of your letter writing.

4. **Visit record.** Record the dates and results of the visits to homes, schools and social settings. Make all entries brief, but complete. This not only will give you a fine record, but will keep you thorough in your program.

Record Page

Beginning date of program _____ Ending date _____

Name of youth _____ Phone _____

Address _____

Prayer Record
Week one _____
Week two _____
Week three _____
Week four _____
Week five _____
Week six _____
Week seven _____
Week eight _____

Phone Record
Week one _____
Week two _____
Week three _____
Week four _____
Week five _____
Week six _____
Week seven _____
Week eight _____

Letter Record

Week one	Week two	Week three	Week four	Week five	Week six	Week seven	Week eight

Visit Record
Home visit
Date_____Description_____
_____
_____
_____

School visit
Date_____Description_____
_____
_____
_____

Social visit
Date_____Description_____
_____
_____
_____

Remember to rotate the groups every eight weeks until all groups have been in each category.

At the end of 32 weeks, 40 youth in your group will have been cared for through prayers, telephone calls, letters and visits. You will know them by name and will have grown closer to them. Your own spiritual life will be enhanced. Your youth group will have a model that may become ritual.

TIME COMPUTATION AND
ADAPTING TO VARIOUS–SIZE GROUPS

All of us have limited time. Some of us work outside of the church and only have a few hours a week that we can dedicate to youth ministry. Others of us are full-time employees of a church and are responsible for youth ministry. The bottom line is that we have just so much time and we must carefully utilize that precious gift.

The 32-week program for the 40 youth computes to 57 minutes 2 seconds a day:

Activities	Minutes a Day
10 youth on the prayer list (3 minutes each) 30 minutes/day	30.00
10 youth on the phone list (3 minutes each) 30 minutes/week	4.29
10 youth on the letter list (10 minutes each) 1 hour and 40 minutes/week	14.29
10 youth on the visit list (45 minutes each) 7 hours and 30 minutes/8 weeks	8.04
Total	57.02

In less than an hour a day, you can conduct a spiritual growth program as all-encompassing as this one for 40 youth. Decide on how much time you have a day and go to it; for example, allow a half-hour for 20 youth, one and one-half hours for 60 youth.

When you first begin this program, try not to involve more than 60 youth. It takes time and discipline for the program to become a part of your life. After this spirituality program becomes a ritual in your life, you may want to involve more than 60 young people. But wait until you have had a few successes to whet your appetite.

If you have limited time or an extra large group, involve counselors or other group leaders in the project. Do not make this a tedious task or drudgery. It should be fun, exciting and rewarding. Half of the worth of the experience is enjoying the growing closeness of the youth and watching the group come together as a Christian community.

For larger groups, divide the youth group into the number of youth leaders who are going to participate. Each leader should take only the number he or she feels comfortable with. Be sure to explain all of the phases of the program and talk about the importance of follow-through. Plan a weekly check-in meeting with those who are participating. It gets lonely out there sometimes, and to be able to check in with others who are participating in this program is vital. The time together can be a sharing experience of ideas to make the program more effective.

A church in south Texas that has more than 300 youth on its roll assigned 60 youth to the youth director and 20 youth to each counselor.

If you divide your group among counselors or other workers, plan to rotate total lists every 32 weeks until each worker has had the opportunity to have each youth on his or her list.

Schedule the 32-week program at least once a year. During the weeks between, focus on other kinds of spirituality programs such as the 30 days of love.

Part of the power of the 32-week spiritual growth program is that it impacts everyone for a focused time and workers do not burn out on it. When you make it an annual event, people look forward to participation.

GOING BEYOND

I recommend that when all of your youth have been through this program, you take a breather. A sense of success upon completion of such a program should be enjoyed, but the program should not be forgotten. Reflect on ways it could become a part of your regular routine and possible ways of introducing the program to others.

As you get to know your kids, you can ask the deeper

questions such as, "How's your walk with the Lord?" and expect honest, seeking answers and questions. Unless youth feel an acceptance by you, the leader, they will not share authentically about their spiritual journey. Build the relationship first, model spirituality, and then challenge youth to "take up the cross and follow."

Epilogue

In a recent conversation with Dr. John Westerhoff, we were discussing the issue of why many youth directors, teachers, counselors, advisors and clergy often leave a church after a short period of time. I was lamenting that some youth workers run out of their "bag of tricks" and move on to another church to get a fresh start, others go back to school for more in-depth study, and others simply "burn out."

John exclaimed, "David, some youth workers move on because they have lost God! Their work is not challenging anymore. They feel used up." That idea clicked. I knew John was right. We cannot be successful in *anything* if we have "lost God."

We must have an ongoing personal spiritual life if we are going to have a relevant ministry. *We simply cannot give what we do not have.* I have shown you model after model of workable programs and projects to help you develop your spiritual growth. I have tried to be deliberate in my approach, yet not presumptuous bending. I am convinced that this principle of "going first" is a cardinal rule and will not change.

I also have reached deep inside of myself and others to present the rationale and procedures for successful, "workable" spiritual growth programs for youth groups.

I am convinced that if this spiritual growth information is absorbed and put to practice, your youth group will become the deep, abiding Christian youth community that you desire *and* your calling to serve God will be fulfilled. My humble prayers go with you.

Peace.

In Christ.

Forever.

Acknowledgments

I thank God for the inspiration, vision and challenge to write **Spiritual Growth in Youth Ministry**.

To write a sentence of thanks to all the people involved in the creation of this project would take a book. I must mention, however, a few special people who have supported me with more than a slap on the back.

Special thanks to: Rose Mary Miller, who stood by me through thin and thick. She prodded me when I needed it and worked through every word on her word processor as we read, recalled and revised.

Lee Sparks, my editor, who was so much more than an editor, or maybe was what a real editor should be. Lee continually encouraged me and made the book a real spiritual pilgrimage for me.

Grantham Couch, my close friend and confidant who believes in me and shows it. So much of my routine nourishment comes from this loving, unselfish friend.

Larry Keefauver and Jim Kolar, two brothers in Christ who have deeply influenced my life and worked with me on many seminars, books, programs and projects. I will be always in their debt. Thanks to them for reading the manuscript, affirming it and making suggestions for improvement.

Also thanks to: Phil Baker, Christy Clark, David Dykes, Ralph Gustafson, Gary Hall, Janie Lyman, Walt Marcum, Pete Mickler, Marshall Monroe, Jack Patrick, Tim Scott, David Torbett, Suzy Yates, Larry Young and many others who tested much of this material, shared with me their own projects and programs and urged the completion of this work.

Answers and Sources for "A Youth Culture Quiz," pp. 14-15.

1. True. "The Connecticut Mutual Life Report on American Values in the '80s: The Impact of Belief" (Harford: The Connecticut Mutual Life Insurance Company, 1981).

2. True. George Gallup Jr. and David Poling, **The Search for America's Faith** (Nashville: Abingdon, 1980).

3. True. "The Connecticut Mutual Life Report."

4. False. George Gallup Jr., "Religion in America 1984" (Princeton: Princeton Religion Research Center, 1984). Only three percent can name all Ten Commandments; 35 percent can name five or more of them

5. True. Ibid.

6. True. **The Search for America's Faith.**

7. True. Ibid.

8. True. Ibid.

9. True. Research by National Association of Secondary School Principals, 1983.

10. True. Ibid.

11. F. **The Search for America's Faith.**

12. E. Ibid.

13. B. This is based on my own experience. "I don't know" allows you to be vulnerable with youth and grow in relationship with them as you search for answers together.

14. B. "Religion in America, 1984" says that 52 percent of youth like the idea of going on religious retreats. In my opinion retreats are the best settings for concentrated doses of spiritual growth.

15. C. **The Search for America's Faith.**

16. F. The best way to recruit leaders is to initiate relationships. That means visiting them.

17. D. Research by National Association of Secondary School Principals, 1983.

18. B. Ibid.

19. C. As you will read many times in this book, you must have a personal spiritual growth program before you can provide authentic spiritual growth programs in youth ministry.

20. A. "Young Adolescents and Their Parents" (Minneapolis: Search Institute, 1984).